Contents

Foreword

This remarkable book comes just in time. The Lutheran church is finally wrestling with the challenge of mission in the United States today—the central issue before it and all the other mainline churches. This book takes its place with a host of resources for those congregations who are feeling a renewed call to evangelism.

Kelly Fryer is persuaded that the Lutheran church has much to offer the searching people of our day. It does not need to dumb-down its tradition, suppress its sacraments, nor adjust itself to the prevailing winds of evangelical America. It should rather cast off self-pity and wake up to use the treasures that it has. She makes a powerful case that within the deepest riches of our own tradition we have the answers for many in our society who are seeking but not finding.

Those many persons looking for an outreach strategy that works with the best and most persuasive concepts and strategies of our tradition will find substantial help here. What may surprise them is the direct and powerful language in which this gospel appeal is made.

There are several echoes of Martin Luther in this book, and not simply in the area of theological content. Kelly Fryer is able to speak with the same fresh directness with which Luther's treatises of 1519 and 1520 spoke to a generation of European Christians who were longing for reform but had almost given up hope for a credible renewal of the church. Fryer has, as he had, a deep sense of her audience and how to communicate with it.

Like Luther, she finds her critical edge not in breaking free from the past, but rather in using its deepest resources to clean out the confusion and debris that had accumulated through the centuries. Like Luther, Fryer's real power comes neither from technique nor even from the strength of the writing, but from that plain speaking that the Word of God alone makes possible.

Some will wonder about her credentials. Many wondered about Luther's authority to challenge the church. In her case the credibility of this book comes not simply from her theological training and clarity, but even more from her rich and exciting experience as a pastor reaching out to the unchurched, building new congregations from the ground up, and leading people not only into membership in the church, but far deeper into active discipleship.

I fear that some may also resent her bluntness. While I cheer for the direct speech of this book, I know that some folks may find her mode of presentation very sharp. I hope they will pause to consider the sharpness of the sources on which she draws—the Bible itself and the Reformation tradition. Over the centuries, every renewal of the church is slowly softened by the passage of time. We need stirring today. Her bold reformulations of reformation themes represent an exciting attempt to cut through the barnacles of time. There is a touch of the prophet in her writing, and the prophets generally sting before they comfort and console.

In that respect I think this book may be of service not only to new Christians who are looking toward the Lutheran church and to pastors and evangelists who are working with them. I think there is a whole secondary audience waiting for this volume—people long gathered in our church who long for a fresh articulation of the gospel.

The truth is that Christian disciples today have to live out their faith in a society that is largely indifferent to what they may believe. To be sure there is little religious persecution of church-goers in the United States. But the great pressures of our society to secure religious peace by making faith a purely private matter has many Christians deeply perplexed about how to live out their convictions in the weekday structures of family, work, and community. There is help here not only for new Lutheran Christians, but for long-time members who need a fresh transfusion of excitement, or even some coaching on how to find words to share what they hold so dear.

It has been a joy to know Pastor Kelly since her first days as a theological student, to watch her transformation from pastor to evangelist, to hear her as an acclaimed speaker throughout our church. This book will take her important witness to more places than any pastor can go, even one with the gifts, the dynamism, and the energy of the author of this book.

TIMOTHY F. LULL
President
Pacific Lutheran Theological Seminary
Berkeley, California

Preface

More than anything, I want to be writing this book for the people in my neighborhood and yours who don't know the great and wonderful God I have come to know in Jesus. I want to share what I have been given with those people out there who are hungry and thirsty for answers and meaning and hope, people who are crying out for direction and searching for love, people who are—some of them—so lost they don't even know it anymore. I want to be able to tell them straight out, in language they will understand, that there is a church here that will welcome them and lead them to the One who makes all the difference. I want them to hear that "church" doesn't have to be a four-letter word. It doesn't have to be a disappointment. It doesn't have to be scary. It doesn't have to be irrelevant. I want to be writing to those people because I know what it's like to be one of them. And my heart breaks for them.

But, instead, I am writing to you.

It will finally be through you—and your church—that all those people meet the God who loves them. It won't be because of some book they read, although that might help a little. It won't be because of a song they hear on the radio, although that can have a powerful impact. It won't be because of an on-line conversation they have in a church-sponsored chat room, although that could open some doors. It will, finally, be because you have invited them face-to-face to come and meet the God you know in Jesus. And it will be because your church welcomed them to the journey of faith where, together, we meet God—or, better yet, are met BY God in the Word and in the Meal, in the Bath, and in the community of God's holy people. You—and you alone—will make the difference.

I know this because you—and your church—have made the difference for me. I wasn't brought up as a Lutheran. Frankly, when I was growing up, I didn't even know what a Lutheran was. But the God I have met through this church—in its teaching and preaching and in the *people* whose lives have been shaped by its history and heritage—is a God who has changed my life.

And, so, this book is a thank offering to God for you. It is my hope and prayer that it will help you think again about what it means to be God's people through Jesus Christ . . . *who also happen to be Lutheran* . . . and that it will help you rediscover why it matters so very much.

I am especially thankful to all those who have helped shape my understanding of what it means to be a *Lutheran* Christian. This includes the theology faculty at Valparaiso University (especially Jim Moore and Dale Lasky, who maybe never knew the impact they had as they endured my arrogance, anger, and doubt); the 1985-1989 faculty at the Lutheran Theological Seminary at Philadelphia; the current faculty at the Lutheran School of Theology in Chicago; all those pastors, far too many to name, who have been mentors and examples for me over the years; the good and faithful people I have been privileged to serve beside and from whom I learned so much at St. Timothy's Lutheran Church (Philadelphia), St. Matthew's Lutheran Church (Kellers Church, Pennsylvania), and Immanuel Lutheran Church (Compton, Illinois); all those who have attended my workshops and seminars, across the country, who ask hard questions and teach me more than I teach them *every single time*; my family-in-law and, especially, Rudy and Jinny Ressmeyer, who in their own time led this church into new and courageous directions and who clung to what it really means to be Lutheran even when that was disputed and dangerous; and the amazing people at Cross of Glory Lutheran Church in Lockport, Illinois—about 70% of whom were not raised Lutherans, either!—but who have dared to adopt the principles in this book, who actually LIVE THEM OUT in ever more innovative ways, and who are crazily committed to changing the world. This book—and all the work we do throughout the church—springs from a vision we share together. I am also thankful to Richard Bliese, Peter Eckart, and Janet Hunt, all of whom read the first draft of this manuscript and gave me a great gift by telling me exactly what they thought of it. But mostly I need to thank my husband, Tim. When his persistent and unconditional love finally melted my heart, it changed everything.

Anything at all that I get "right" in this book is because of the hard work, clear thinking, deep faith, and loving example of all these people. But I alone will claim anything that I get wrong. And I give them permission to tell me so. Let the conversation begin.

Introduction:
Of Traffic Jams
& Transformation

I used to listen to the radio every morning as I was brushing my teeth. And, because I live in a metropolitan area, about every 10 minutes or so they break in with a weather forecast and traffic report. Which is fine and dandy on the *other* six days of the week. But on Sundays I just don't want to hear it. I don't even turn it on anymore. Monday through Friday the traffic report sounds like this: "If you're supposed to be at work by nine, I hope you've left your house by now . . . it's bad out there!" Even Saturdays usually have something exciting happening out on the roads. There's a football game or a street fair or a big sale at the mall or some other event that has people up and out early. But not on Sundays. Nobody goes anywhere on Sundays. Sundays are dead.

The last thing Jesus did, according to Luke anyway, was to share a vision of what might one day happen: " . . . you will receive power when the Holy Spirit has come upon you; and you will be my witnesses in Jerusalem, in all Judea and Samaria, and to the ends of the earth" (Acts 1:8).

And Isaiah had a similar vision before Jesus ever even came along: "In days to come the mountain of the LORD's house shall be established as the highest of the mountains, and shall be raised above the hills; all the nations shall stream to it. Many peoples shall come and say, 'Come, let us go up the mountain of the LORD, to the house of the God of Jacob; that he may teach us his ways and that we may walk in his paths" (Isaiah 2:2-3).

I have a vision of my own. Cars backed up for miles, bumper to bumper on a Sunday morning. And that guy in the traffic update helicopter hovering overhead, reporting happily from the sky, "Well, folks, if you're on your way to a nine o'clock service this morning, I sure hope you've already left your house. It's madness out there!"

This is a vision I know I share with MANY people in the Church, throughout my denomination—the Evangelical Lutheran Church in America (ELCA)—and across every other mainline Protestant church. We want our congregations to be vibrant, growing places that make a difference in people's lives and in the world. We want to do what Jesus asked us to do. But we don't see it happening. It isn't true everywhere, of course, but in too many mainline churches, we see declining worship attendance and decreasing (aging) membership rolls. We see depressed pastors and angry congregational members. We feel like we've "tried everything," and nothing is making a difference.

I know what it's like to be in a struggling congregation. In fact, in November 1992, when I accepted the call to serve as pastor at Cross of Glory Lutheran Church, that 13-year-old congregation, like so many, was dying. Today it is not. In fact, thanks be to God, worship attendance has grown by nearly 500% in the past 10 years. And 75% of our new members hadn't been part of a faith community of any kind since they were children . . . if ever . . . until they came to Cross of Glory. About that many weren't raised Lutheran, either. The place has new energy now, and a vision, and a willingness to follow Jesus wherever he leads. But none of this happened because of the way we *did* things. In fact, a lot of us in this denomination are discovering that just DOING things differently doesn't matter at all.

In a recent study, the ELCA's Department for Research and Evaluation looked specifically at some of the "techniques" that most people think you would just have to use if you want your church to grow. For example, they looked at what happened to churches with contemporary worship services. (They use drums!)

Now, I like drums myself. When I was in junior high, I wanted to BE Karen Carpenter. And I might just be the only female Lutheran minister in the country who can sometimes be found preaching the sermon *and* playing the drums in the band at church on Sunday mornings. I would rather go to a church that *rocks* any week of the year than one that doesn't. But the truth is, when it comes to whether or not a church grows, having drums or not having them pretty much doesn't matter. In fact, there was no single "technique" that DID make a difference over the past decade. At least not in our denomination. It didn't matter what our newsletters looked like or how often we knocked on doors inviting people to church or how much people liked the pastor's sermons. There was—*get ready*—only ONE factor that was a good predictor for whether or not a church grew: The ONLY factor that really matters is whether or not a church has a clear enough vision of where God wants it to go that it is willing to do whatever it takes to follow wherever God leads.[1]

---

[1] After studying the results of a "decade of evangelism" and evaluating growing ELCA congregations across the United Satates, the Department for Research and Evaluation of the ELCA concluded: "It is reasonable to believe that evangelism, contemporary worship, and media advertising will have a direct impact on average worship attendance; yet, this is not the case if the congregation is without a clear sense of mission and purpose with the welcoming of innovation and change. This suggests that an ethos must first be developed wherein the congregation captures a sense of a clear mission and purpose and welcomes innovation and change before evangelism, changes in styles of worship, or establishing a media campaign have an impact." The results of two important studies are summarized in *An Evaluation of the 1991 Evangelism Strategy*, Ken W. Inskeep, October 3, 2000, www.elca.org/re/reports/evan1991.pdf, and *Worship Attendance in the Evangelical Lutheran Church in America: Faith Communities Today*, Ken W. Inskeep and Jeffrey L. Drake, November 2000, www.elca.org/re/reports/ccspwrsp1.pdf.

How we do things *does* matter. But that's not the real issue. The real issue is who we ARE. Are we people who are so confident in God's love and grace that we are able to try new things and welcome new people and embrace new ideas and dream new dreams? Are we clear enough about

> **Vibrant & growing churches have this in common: They have a clear sense of vision, and they are open to change.**

what we are being called to do and to be that we are willing to set off on whatever new adventure God calls us to? Are we full of enough hope that we can dare to fail, to risk messing everything up, to take the chance that we are wrong? Are we free to love, to serve, to share, to sing, to laugh, to lead, to give ourselves away? Are we willing to let ourselves be turned upside-down and inside-out by a God who wants for us, for our congregations, and for our world more than anything we could ever even ask or imagine? Who ARE we? Who are YOU? How is your life being changed by God's power and presence and call? How is God changing your congregation? These are the real questions. And this is the place to begin.

Not long ago, when I was having one of those "Is EVERYBODY around me just an idiot, or what?!?" weeks, I was complaining to a friend of mine about how *nothing* was going right *anywhere*. I was dealing with crabby people at church, my husband was crabby, my kids were crabby, my schoolmates were crabby, strangers at the grocery store were crabby, people in traffic were crabby. You name it.

"Every time I turn around," I whined, "it just gets worse!"

Tana listened patiently for a while (probably waiting for me to tell her she was being crabby, too). And then, in a courageous whisper she said: "Kelly . . ."

"Whaaat?" I said cautiously. I knew something I didn't want to hear was coming next.

"Do you notice what all of those people have in common?"

Silence.

"You," she said.

I hate it when I have to look at myself first when I'd rather just look around for somebody else to blame for the mess I'm in. The impulse to finger point is as old as, well, Adam and Eve. "She told me to eat it!" he said. "But the snake gave it to me in the first place!" she said. It's so much harder to accept responsibility for things when they've gone wrong than it is to dump it on somebody else. One season, Frank Thomas is a hero to his teammates and anybody who's paying attention in the windy city because the White Sox are on the road to victory, and the very next season he's a bum because the Sox can't catch a break. We all sometimes need a courageous friend to whisper in our unwilling ears: "Hey there. You know I love you. But maybe the problem is you."

We may not want to hear it, but God's transformation of the Church—and of our congregations—will not come through some secret, fail-safe, "see-it-at-a-conference" or "read-it-in-a-book" technique that you can take home, mix with water, bake in a 350-degree oven, and serve to your people. God's transformation of the congregation I am part of will begin with ME . . . and my heart and my mind and my life. And God's transformation of the congregation you are part of will begin with YOU. My good friend, Dave, reminds me at every turn: *Changed people change churches.* There simply is no other way.

Some of us really have "tried everything." Maybe we have needed to do this. And at some point, maybe some of those things we are trying will turn out to be really great ideas! Techniques *can* and *do* work in congregations where the Spirit of God has created an openness to change. The way we worship, how well we use our newsletters and Web sites, how we are organized, the kinds of programming we offer, what our buildings look like, whether or not we have a catchy mission statement—all of these things DO make a difference. And there are all *kinds* of experts out there who really do know this stuff and to whom we should be listening. But they are NOT the place to start. We need to begin by remembering who we are.

This will happen as we turn to Scripture and to our theological tradition. This will happen as we turn to one another in meaningful and lively conversation. This will happen as we turn to God in prayer. *And it will happen only as each one of us takes responsibility for doing these things.*

What God wants for us more than anything is to turn our darkness into light, to make whole what has been broken, to fill us—and our congregations—up with joy and hope and new life. God wants us to be healthy and strong so that we reach a world that desperately needs what we have already been given. Isn't that what God meant in Genesis 12:2, when he told Abraham and Sarah, "You have been blessed *so that* you can be a blessing"? Isn't that what Jesus was really saying in Matthew 5:14-16, when he told us that we have been "lit up" by the love and the power of God *so that* we can light up the whole world?

I believe it is God's vision, too, to finally see a traffic jam on Sunday morning.

1

In Defense of Dogma

For the time is coming when people will not put up with sound doctrine, but having itching ears, they will accumulate for themselves teachers to suit their own desires, and will turn away from listening to the truth and wander away to myths.

   Paul, writing to his friend Timothy
   2 Timothy 4:3-4

You've got to be careful if you don't know where you're going 'cause you might not get there.

   Yogi Berra
   The Yogi Book, Workman Publishing, 1998

Dogma: What a *mean*-sounding word. Maybe that's why Lutherans have never really used it. We Lutherans have the Augsburg "Confession" (a nice little word that almost sounds like we're apologizing for it) and the Small "Catechism" (which is rather dusty, as if it belongs in a class on ancient history, but doesn't necessarily sound very scary). Dogma, on the other

---

dog·ma   (n. pl. dog·mas or dog·ma·ta)

1. A doctrine relating to matters such as morality and faith, set forth in an authoritative manner by a church.

2. An authoritative principle, belief, or statement of ideas and opinion—especially one considered to be absolutely true.

---

hand, conjures up images of shadowy, looming, authority figures standing over straight rows of students cowering under the threat of a whack by an old wooden ruler: Believe this or else. Pretty nasty stuff.

At best, Dogma is the name of your least favorite aunt, the one who pinched you really hard on the cheek when she said hello and gave you a lecture, when she said goodbye, about maybe having better manners "next time." The one who always gave you underwear for Christmas and heavy, woolen socks that itched and made your feet sweat even in the winter. "Please, Aunt Dogma," you want to scream, "loosen that bun!"

Well, hold on just a darn minute. Do you remember what your dad would say as soon as that aunt of yours would leave? "Come on now, kids," he'd apologize, his eyes smiling mischievously, like he knew something we didn't. "Remember. She means well." And, I sort of hate to admit it now, but he was right. She did.

I'm going to go out on a limb here and say that maybe what some of us—and our congregations—need is a heavy dose of good, old-fashioned dogma. Dogma is, simply defined, a set of principles that we believe to be true. It is a "head" thing, not a "heart" thing. And a lot of us, before we do anything else, need to get our heads on straight. *We need to know what we think*—about God and about our faith, about the world and about ourselves, and about what it means to say that we are the *church* and that we have a job to do. We need to know who we are. In fact, until we are really clear about these things, we will find ourselves "wandering" around, as Paul warned, from one *myth* . . . one half-truth . . . one info-commercial promise . . . one talk show host's advice . . . one church-growth guru's latest list of things every church just HAS to do . . . to another. And we will be as lost as we can be.

Been there, done that

I actually know quite a lot about being lost, not only in my personal life, which is a whole other story, but as the pastor of a church that has had to figure this stuff out. If you are a member or, God bless you, a *leader* in your church, you may be able to relate to some of this story.

But, first, a warning: Some parts of this story may make you feel uncomfortable . . . for all kinds of reasons. It raises what has become a very important and painful issue in the life of our church. And, whichever side of this issue you stand on, you are probably not going to like what happened here. I'm going to tell you about it anyway because it changed *everything*. This is a story about how one congregation—and one young pastor—came face to face with the consequences of not having their heads on straight, of not being clear enough about who they are and what they believe. This story helps clarify exactly why Aunt Dogma is such an important part of the family.

The story begins in November 1992, when there were about 60 people worshiping at Cross of Glory Lutheran Church on a typical Sunday morning. The congregation had a $40,000 budget deficit. And they owed more on their little building THEN than they did when they built it 10 years before. It was kind of a mess. But the folks in that congregation wanted to see their church live again. And so they decided to start over.

They knocked on doors inviting neighbors to worship. They changed worship to make it more accessible to people who didn't have a lot of church experience. They started some new programs that were designed to be helpful to people in town who didn't have a church home. They found a good sale on some church "marketing" material from an old campaign that was being discontinued, and bought all the bumper stickers and door hangers they could get their hands on. That's how they became "The Welcome Place." And they really tried to be. They did a pretty good job of getting the message out and, in the first year, welcomed over 150 new members. Most of those new people didn't even know what a Lutheran was before they came, and many of them had never been part of ANY faith community. You would think, wouldn't you, that all this would have made those original 60 people happy. It did . . . for a while.

But, pretty soon, there were "new" people sitting in the "old" people's seats. And sitting at the church council table. And leading worship. And changing everything. And those original 60 people got mad. They got so mad that within two years most of them left the church . . . and a lot of those new people left, too. Who wants to be part of a church that is fighting all the time?

I wish I could say that, as the new pastor at Cross of Glory back in those days, I did everything right. I didn't. In fact, I was so taken by surprise by how MAD everyone got that I didn't know what to do. I was young and, well, just really dumb. And I did every single wrong thing a pastor could do in the middle of a situation where everyone is feeling unhappy and sad. In fact, I think I made up some *new* wrong stuff to do.

But, somehow God manages to get things done even when we seem bound and determined to mess it all up. God raised up new leaders who had a vision for where God was taking that congregation. A buyer was found for the little, debt-ridden building. A public school gym was rented for weekend worship services. A search began for a new building site. Before long, new people started coming again . . . all kinds of new people . . . including David and Tina.[2]

And this is when things got *really* interesting.

David and Tina were from an "independent" Christian church background and identified themselves as evangelical

---

[2] Actually, these aren't their real names. Many of the names in this book aren't real. But the stories are. They are as real as they can be.

fundamentalists. They knew the Bible pretty well and were comfortable talking about their faith. In fact, they looked and sounded a lot like experts, and they quickly came to be considered leaders in the church. I'm still not sure what brought them in. Maybe because I preach from the Bible every Sunday, we fooled them. I have no idea how they figured they would deal with having a woman pastor. And it was only a matter of time before they started asking questions about why we were baptizing babies and having Holy Communion so often. Mostly, I tried to dodge these questions. The last thing I wanted, after everything we had been through, was more fighting.

But it all came to a head around the time Susan and Joan started worshiping with us. These two women shared a small, quiet home in town. And, although it was apparently obvious to everyone else at church except me, they were a couple. It seems *they* were fooled by our "Welcome Place" logo, which features a cute little church with a *rainbow* in the doorway.[3] It took me a couple of weeks to hear the gossip at the coffee pot after worship. "Psst . . . what are we going to tell our kids?!?" people were saying. "What are we going to do if they want to become members???"

And me? I managed to dodge these questions, too. I was just happy to have people in the seats again.

Then, one Sunday after worship, David and Tina handed me a letter. It said: "If you don't do something about those two women, we are going to leave this church. And other people will follow us."

"Shoot," I thought. "Now what am I going to do?"

And, then, not five minutes later, Susan and Joan came over to see me. They handed me a letter, too. And their letter said this:

---

[3] A rainbow is one of the symbols often associated with the gay and lesbian community. I didn't know this at the time, of course, and neither did any of the people in my congregation. Well, no one said anything, anyway. Maybe those who DID know were hoping we knew, too, and actually meant it.

"Thank you for welcoming us. We like you and we like this church. But we know that our presence here is creating a problem. And so we are not going to come back."

Two letters in five minutes. I spent the rest of the day stewing and then did what every brave pastor would do. I called the church council together for a meeting, read both letters aloud and said, "You have to do something about this."

We talked about this situation for a long time. We talked so long that, now, I'm a little embarrassed about it. Finally, Mike, who had been one of the coffee-pot conversation leaders, said, "Wait a minute. Whatever else might be true, we are THE WELCOME PLACE. Right? Isn't that what all our signs say? And doesn't that mean everyone is welcome here?"

Mike's question changed everything. Thanks to a good sale on a soon-to-be discontinued marketing campaign—and a blast of lucidity that came, I believe, straight from the Holy Spirit—we had somehow, to our surprise, discovered that we had an identity. We had, it seemed, some small sense of who we were. And it made all the difference.

So with not a lot—but enough—clarity, the church council did what every brave church council would do. They said, "Kelly, you have to go talk to these people." So I did. I sat down with David and Tina and said, "OK, look. We aren't going to agree about everything. There may even be some really big things we never all agree on. But YOU ARE WELCOME HERE." And then I talked with Susan and Joan. I told them, "Look, we aren't all always going to agree about everything. There may even be some really big things we never all agree on. But YOU ARE WELCOME HERE." David and Tina left the church . . . and, in fact, there were a couple of other families that followed them. Susan and Joan stayed. Joan even joined the choir.

This was a defining moment in my ministry, and in the life of this congregation. It became painfully clear that unless we know who we are and what we're all about, we are going to find ourselves in one big mess after another. This situation clarified how important it is for us to know what we *think* about things. It made us realize that, like her or not, we *need* Aunt Dogma . . . tight little bun and all.

Turn your head

So, *do* you know who you are . . . and what you stand for? If you're like a lot of people I know, you may not be sure how to answer that question. Some of us are pretty clear about what we DON'T believe. But we would be stumped if somebody asked us to sum up what we DO. And this is true for those of us who are church members, too. It isn't that we don't *have* strong beliefs. It's just that we would have a hard time saying exactly what our beliefs are. For example, when I ask Lutherans across the country what they think it means to be a Christian, much less a Christian who also happens to be a Lutheran, I get all kinds of interesting responses including everything from "We're saved by grace!" to Jell-O. And we are not, by any means, the only Christians who are struggling with this issue.

Copyright © Grimmy, Inc. Reprinted with special permission of King Features Syndicate.

In fact, this has been a problem in the Christian community for as long as anybody can remember. You might know that the apostle Paul clashed with the apostle Peter for floating in the wind and refusing to take a firm stand on the biggest issue of their day. The controversy back then was about whether or not you had to be *Jewish* before you became a follower of Jesus. For a while, Peter said, "No, you don't." He accepted those who weren't Jewish and even ate with them, like family. But Jesus' brother, James, disagreed. He thought you had to be Jewish first. And, when some of James's friends saw what Peter was doing, Peter got scared and stopped doing it. He knew James would never approve. And Peter was afraid he'd get in trouble. That's why when he came to Antioch, Paul shouted, "I opposed him to his face, because he stood self-condemned!" (Galatians 2:11). Stand somewhere!, Paul challenged Peter. Know who you are!

And, as mad as Paul was at Peter, he was even angrier with the members of the churches in the part of his world called "Galatia." The early Christians there were wandering so far away from their central beliefs that they appeared to forget they ever even had any. Paul wanted them to remember that at the heart of their life as Christians was a message of grace through *faith*. "I am astonished!" Paul yelled, "that you are so quickly deserting the one who called you in the grace of Christ and are turning to a different gospel" (Galatians 1:6) This isn't about what YOU do, he reminded them. This is about what GOD has done, through Christ. He was furious with his friends in Galatia . . . and, even more so, with those who had gotten them off track. "I wish those who unsettle you would castrate themselves!" he barked (Galatians 5:12).

Paul was generally an excitable guy. But he was right on the money when he said that knowing who you are and what you stand for is important. And there might not be a more important thing for those of us who are Christians—who also happen to be Lutheran—to be thinking about today.

It is no secret that a lot of churches are in trouble. Congregations —especially "mainline" Protestant ones, like Lutherans—are getting smaller. And the membership rolls are getting older. Some people want to say this is because our worship services are boring and the music is too old-fashioned. Well, it just isn't that simple. While lots of growing churches have found it important to figure out how to worship in a way that sounds "contemporary," there are plenty of growing churches across the country that have retained the rich "tradition" of our historical roots. Some churches are experimenting with "fusing" the two together. The point is that healthy churches don't have a particular worship style, or any other single characteristic activity, in common. They don't all deliver bread to newcomers in their community. They don't all have dynamic preachers. They don't all have small group Bible studies. They are not all located in growing communities. The only thing vibrant, healthy congregations have in common is that they know who they are and who God is calling them to be. And they are so clear about it that they are willing to do whatever it takes to be faithful to that call.

In other words, they have their heads on straight.

Not long ago, I met a woman who helped me understand the importance of paying attention to where your head is. She is a theologian. But, more to the point, she is a martial-arts expert. And she has that very calm presence about her that people do who know they can take you out in a second if you make a wrong move. "I have learned something very important from the martial arts," she said. "If your head hits the floor, your body will follow." Then she drove it home: "So, if you want your body to go some-where . . . turn your head."

In other words, our actions will be informed by the principles that guide our thinking. Where the head leads, the body will follow. What we DO as God's people through Jesus—and what we do as the church together—has to start with a solid understanding of who we ARE. It begins with knowing what we *think* about things. It means having a grasp on what we believe to be true about ourselves and about God and about our life together as Christians. For those of us who are Lutherans, it also means being clear about what it means to *be* Lutheran.

If our congregations are struggling, it is most likely because they are struggling with this issue. We're not entirely sure who we are. And, if our congregations are struggling with this issue, it is in large part because WE are struggling. Nothing will change in our churches unless it changes in us. Our congregations will have clarity when WE have it. It is my responsibility and yours to figure this stuff out together; to think seriously about what it means to say that we are Christians . . . who also happen to be Lutheran; to explore the depths of Scripture and the richness of our theological tradition and to remember who we are.

I know it sounds a lot like something dear old Aunt Dogma would say, but I really think: We have some serious work to do.

Wrestling with the Word

1. Nehemiah was working as a "cupbearer" to King Artaxerxes, far from home, when he heard that his people were in trouble. They were back living in Jerusalem after a long exile, but the wall around the city had not been rebuilt. And they were in danger. He knew he had to DO something about this. But he did something else first. What was it? What difference do you think it made? Read Nehemiah 1:1-4.

2. Jesus knew he was headed for trouble in Jerusalem, and he wanted to get his disciples ready for it. Right before he told them about what was coming—both for himself AND for them—and that they, too, would have to "take up a cross" and

follow him, Jesus asked a very important question. This question forced Peter to clearly articulate what it is he believed to be true. What was that question? And what was Peter's response? What difference do you think Jesus' question makes today . . . and in the years to come? Read Matthew 16:13-16.

Thinking things over

1. When was the last time you had a really important decision to make? What were the most important factors that went into making it? Who did you talk to? What resources did you use? How did you feel about the outcome?

2. How possible is it for a whole group of people—a family, say, or a congregation, or a *country!*—to agree on "the most important things"? What difference does it, or can it make, when a group shares a clear set of beliefs in common?

3. Is it more important to THINK first and then act? Or the other way around? Why? Which are you more likely to do?

4. Describe a time when you were involved in a conflict with someone you love . . . and you later realized that what you were fighting about didn't really matter that much after all? What would have happened if, in the heat of the argument, someone had remembered the "big" picture . . . and all of the important things you have in common? How would it have made a difference?

Talking it over

Dear God, it is so easy to get confused about what really matters. Forgive us when we get ourselves turned around. Help us seek your direction. Make things clear for us. Be with us as we take a stand, prayerfully, so that we can be your people in this world. We know that the job before us is huge and important. Help us get ready to do it. In Jesus' name. Amen

2

A Confession

For I am the least of the apostles, unfit to be called an apostle, because I persecuted the church of God. But by the grace of God I am what I am.

≪ Paul, writing to his friends in Corinth
1 Corinthians 15:9-10

I am a sinner, and I am aware of my sin; for I have not yet put off my flesh, to which sin will cling as long as it lives. But I will obey the Spirit rather than the flesh. That is, by faith and hope I will take hold of Christ.

≪ Martin Luther, *Concerning the Ministry*, 1523

We have our work cut out for us. And, in hopes of being helpful, I am ready to take a stab at providing a framework for the rest of our conversation together about what it means to be a *Lutheran* Christian. But I'm feeling the need, before I go any further, to make a confession. Like another—indeed, the most famous Lutheran we know—I grew up in a Roman Catholic home. Martin Luther was a Catholic, too.

And, as it was for him, the church was a very important part of my younger years. In fact, I loved the church. I loved the musty way the church smelled when I walked in and the way the old wooden pews creaked beneath me when I sat down. I loved the rhythm of people praying together and the solemn silence that settled over us when the Word was read. I loved the idea that I was somehow holy enough to receive my Lord as he met me at the Table each week, even though in all the rest of my life I was "just a kid." It made me feel important.

A lot of the most important people in my life have been Catholic, too. My parents, for example, who made sure we got to church even by sled, if necessary, like in THE BIG CHICAGO STORM of '67. And my aunts—Hazel, May, and Gen. Actually, they were my *grandmother's* aunts. They were so old! And they were wonderful. I would stay with them once in a while during long summer days in a rustic Indiana farmhouse. And I would always get to sleep in the big, creaky featherbed in my Aunt Gen's room. I would go in early and fidget until Gen came in. The room would be dark, and she would think I was asleep. She would quietly get herself ready for bed and then kneel down to say her nightly prayers. The moonlight would stream in so that I could just make out the outline of her bowed head. She would pray the rosary. And then came the best part, when she would make up her own prayers. I will never forget the sound of her voice praying for me. She prayed that I would grow up to be confident and strong, and that I would love the Lord and know that there was a plan for my life. I suspect she knew all along that I was awake, listening in the dark. But she probably never knew what a mark she left on me. Her faithfulness is part of the reason I am here today.

At some point, though—and I won't give you all the gory details —I became deeply disappointed in the church. And I was really, really mad at God. For 10 years I stormed against anything even resembling "organized" religion. I wasn't an atheist, although I would have probably told you that I was. The fact is, you can't hate something you don't believe in. And I *hated* God. I invested a lot of energy in convincing everybody I knew who DID believe in God that they were stupid. And the outrageous way in which I lived my life was my way of telling God to stick it in his ear. I was selfish and self-destructive. I did and said and WAS things I am too embarrassed to tell you about now.

But then, one day, I met a young man who was somehow able to see through all that. I don't know how. It was a miracle.

He somehow saw through the anger and the arrogance, through the self-centeredness and spitefulness, and through the pain . . . to see something worth loving, something beautiful and holy and whole. He saw what God sees. And, in his eyes, I began to see it, too. This young man was not only a Lutheran; he was an S.O.B.—*son of a bishop*. He had spent his whole life drinking from a deep well of love and forgiveness and mercy. He had never known that it could be any other way. His church made him the man he is, gave him eyes to see what God sees. And he was not afraid to tell me that. His love changed me. And so did his witness. I fell in love with him. In fact, I married him. And it didn't take long, either, for me to fall in love with the God he knew in Jesus, the One who had been made real for him in the community of faith that takes its name from a former Catholic named Martin.

The bottom line is, it was grace that drew me into this church . . . and it is grace that keeps me here.

A definition

Grace is at the heart of the best sort of "bottom line" definition I have ever heard of what it means to be a Lutheran. I wish I could tell you from whom I first heard this definition. But I can't. I don't remember. The way I do recall it, through the fog of personal mythology that sometimes develops as time goes by, is that he was a visiting professor on campus my first year of seminary. And, forgive me, he was just not holding my attention this particular day. It was a *beautiful* day on campus and I wanted to be outside playing. Instead, I sat in the amphitheater with my classmates, listening to a lecture about some long-dead theologian. I was bored. And I don't think I was alone. He must have known that we weren't listening because he suddenly slapped his notebook shut and stopped talking. He wasn't going to waste one more breath on us. But, before he left the room, he picked up a

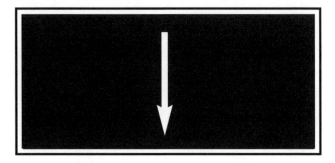

piece of chalk and went to the board. He drew a gigantic ARROW, pointing straight down, stood back, and said: "If you understand that, you understand everything you need to know about what it means to be a Christian . . . who also happens to be a Lutheran." And then he left the room.

We just sat there staring at it, this enormous, stark ARROW pointing straight down. And then I thought the most logical thing I could think, given everything that had just happened, "*He thinks we're all going to hell.*"

The next time we gathered for class, he began by drawing that same arrow on the board. This time, as he began to speak, he had our full attention. "Here's what this means," he said. "God always comes down. God *always* comes down. There is never *anything* that we can ever do to turn that arrow around and make our way UP to God. God came down in Jesus. And God still comes down, in the bread and in the wine, in the water and in the fellowship of believers. God ALWAYS comes down."

The starting point

Somebody gave me a T-shirt recently that said, in bold letters, "ymbali!" I thought, at first, it was a fun, new African expression, something along the lines of "Hakuna Matata," from Disney's *The Lion King*, which means "Don't Worry!" I was amused when I looked at the back of the shirt to see that, in fact, "ymbali" stands for "you might be a Lutheran if . . ." Then there was a whole list of things many Lutherans can probably relate to. For example: You might be a Lutheran if . . . when someone in the *Star Wars* movie says, "May the force be with you," YOU say, "And also with you!"

The truth is, MOST of the things that many of us associate with being "Lutheran" are, when you come right down to it, nothing but *adiaphora* (a-dee-A-fora). If you don't know any other Latin words, this is one you'll want to be able to use. Those church leaders who led the Reformation in Europe 500 years ago used this word to help people sort out the things that really matter from the things that don't. They had to decide what to do, for example—now that they were *Lutherans*—about all the traditions and rituals they were used to keeping as Catholics. Should we fast during Lent or shouldn't we? Should we have statues in our churches or not? That sort of thing. And they decided that anything that helps people meet the God who always comes down, is IN; anything that absolutely gets in the way of that is OUT; and everything else is *adiaphora*. It just doesn't matter all that much.

Interestingly, the Tenth Article of the Formula of Concord—a pretty important document for Lutherans—is called *Concerning Ecclesiastical Practices*, and it is subtitled *Which Are Called Adiaphora or Indifferent Matters.*[4] Lutheran churches engaged in various ceremonies and practices that were not commanded or forbidden by God's Word in Scripture. Writers of the Formula said that such ceremonies and practices were not "worship ordained by God," but churches had the freedom to create and

---

[4]   From *The Book of Concord: The Confessions of the Lutheran Church*, eds. Robert Kolb and Timothy J. Wengert (Minneapolis: Fortress Press, 2000 edition), p. 515.

change them to suit their particular situation, and for "good order and decorum." In other words, even back then, it was clear that a lot of the rituals and practices that make up our life together as church just aren't that critical. *They* are not what really matters.

And yet, in our day, there appears to be some confusion over what is essential to our understanding of what it means to be Christians who are also Lutheran . . . and what is not essential. I don't know how else to understand the fights we have over what color hymnal we should use or even what kind of music we sing during worship. It is possible, I think, that sometimes we are guilty—without meaning to be—of letting things like culture and tradition get in the way of our seeing clearly to the "bottom line" of what it means to be Lutheran. Not that culture and tradition aren't important. They are. But they aren't the ONLY things. And they certainly are not the most important things. Sometimes fresh eyes can help.

If, for example, I am messing around with how to redecorate my house, where to put certain pieces

Common answers to the question:
What does it mean to be a Lutheran?

Saved by grace!

Word and Sacrament

Priesthood of all believers

We know how to SING!

(And we sing ALL the verses!)

Pot luck dinners & Jell-O

"We've never done it that way before!"

Liturgical worship

Theology of the cross

We're German

No we're not. We're Norwegian!

Quilts

What color hymnal do YOU like best?

Coffee hours

Small Catechism

Lake Wobegon

"We're not Catholics"

"We're not Baptists, either!"

of furniture, how to hang pictures in a new way, I might ask a friend to come over to help me. She doesn't have to be an expert. But she will bring fresh eyes. She hasn't been looking at the same furniture and the same pictures in the same place, day after day after day. She'll be able, maybe, to be a little more creative, a little more imaginative. She'll suggest things I hadn't thought about.

Frankly, maybe it takes people who are essentially "outsiders" to see through the clutter of our cultures and traditions, to the heart of things. For example, I was in a group of rather diverse Lutherans not long ago. Each group, including African-Americans and Asian-Americans and American Indians and all kinds of other people from across the country, talked about how hard it is to be Lutheran in a church that is so predominantly white, middle class, and "northern European." After several hours of listening to their stories, I finally asked the question others must have had but didn't dare say out loud.

"Given everything you've just said," I asked, "why in the world would you want to BE Lutheran?"

They looked at me like I was crazy. And then, one after another, they gave an answer that could have sprung from my own heart. "No other church," they said, "is so clear about a God who loves me just as I am. No other church is so clear about what it means to be saved, not because of anything that I do or AM, but by grace through faith alone."

In other words, Lutherans know, down in their souls, that God always comes down. God comes down to meet us when we are rich and when we are poor, when we are black and when we are white, when we are broken and when we are whole. God comes DOWN because none of us, not one, could ever do anything that would make us worthy enough to make our way UP to God. God comes down to *set us free* from every single thing that binds us and burdens us and holds us back from being the people we have been created and called to be. God comes down

to set us free us from sin and death and the power of the evil. [5]
God comes down to set us free to love and to laugh and to learn
and to give ourselves away.

The apostle Paul wrote that at the "right time," while we were
still weak and lost in our sin, Christ died for us (Romans 5:6-8).
Jesus came *down* here and went to the cross for us, so that we
could be free enough to live again. In this crazy way, God "proves
his love for us!" It was this wonderful truth that Martin Luther
and the Reformers rediscovered 500 years ago. And, frankly, this
truth is the thing that mattered most to them. It is the bottom
line of what it means to be a Lutheran. It is the framework for
everything else we say and do and are. It is the starting point.

Five guiding principles

In the aftermath of the "Two Letter Incident" (pages 19-22),
our church council decided that we really needed to put some
energy into clarifying who and what we are as a congregation. We
spent a lot of time talking about the things that are important to
us. And we agreed that when it comes to the resources we would
use to answer the question "Who are we?" that the scriptures had
to be first on that list. The ancient creeds were there, too. So were
the Lutheran Confessions and our rich theological heritage as
heirs of those 16th-century Protestant Reformers. And we agreed
that the framework for the whole conversation would be our
understanding of the God who always comes down to set us free.

The result of this effort was a set of core *values* . . . essential
beliefs . . . or, what came to be called, "guiding principles." These
five guiding principles were short enough that they could be easily
remembered and so simple that even our children could under-

---

[5] Commenting on the benefits God gives in Baptism, Martin Luther said:
"In Baptism God forgives sin, delivers from death and the devil, and gives
everlasting salvation to all who believe what he has promised" (*The Small
Catechism.* Minneapolis: Augsburg Fortress, 1979 edition).

stand them. They have become part of the very blood stream of this congregation. They may look simple. But, in fact, these principles provide direction at every turning point and help in every disagreement. They are posted on every classroom wall and planted in the heart of every leader. Each of these five guiding principles could, I think, be affirmed and accepted by every Christian. But we believe they are, put together in this way, what makes us uniquely *Lutheran*. In fact, if you are a Lutheran, I suspect they will be strangely familiar to you even if you have never seen them like this before. They will seem to *you* somehow right and true.

1. **Jesus Is Lord**
2. **Everyone Is Welcome**
3. **Love Changes People**
4. **Everybody Has Something to Offer**
5. **The World Needs What We Have**

At the same time, I should warn you that these five may or may not be universal principles. We have entered a brave new world where many people, perhaps rightly, believe there is no longer any such thing as a "universal" truth. And, to be sure, these five principles have, in countless ways, been shaped by the cultural and socioeconomic context within which we, the people in this particular congregation and I, live. These principles are, without a doubt, shaped by the fact that most of us here at Cross of Glory are "outsiders," having come to Lutheranism by choice and not by birth. These five principles describe the way we understand things from where *we* stand. And you, perhaps, stand in a much different place.

I hope, in fact, that instead of just accepting these five principles, you will wrestle with them. Test them. Restate them. Add to them. Come to your own conclusions, on the basis of how you read Scripture and understand our rich tradition, of what it means for *you*, in your place, to be God's people in Christ.

From where we stand, however, these five guiding principles, put together in this particular way, are a full and clear summary of what is uniquely Lutheran. They are like part of our Lutheran genetic code, the DNA of renewal and revitalization. We believe they articulate clearly what is essential. We believe these principles are faithful to the Scriptures and to our confessional heritage. This is our way of answering the question "Who are we?"

And so, as another "new" Lutheran once more or less said, knowing how risky it would be to stick his neck out, we say with confidence and in hopefulness that it will be helpful, "Here we stand."

Wrestling with the Word

1. The Christians in Rome didn't like one another very much. Some of them had been raised in the Jewish faith. Some of them were pagans. Paul needed their help before he left on what he hoped would be a great missionary trip to Spain. The letter he wrote to them was an effort to get them to see that what they had in common as Christians was "the gospel," the good news of God who CAME DOWN in Jesus to set us free. He wanted them to willingly let go of all the cultural and traditional stuff that was getting in the way of their ability to move forward in mission, and embrace the "bottom line." Read Romans 3:21-28. What was the bottom line, as far as Paul was concerned?

2. It may surprise you to know that Martin Luther's rediscovery of the God who always comes down, who is merciful and loving even when we are not, began as he read the Old Testament and, particularly, as he prayed through the Psalms. Many of these psalms are attributed to David, who was king in Israel

and who did many great things for his people but who also
made some really big mistakes. Yet, he knew that, even in his
sin and weakness, God would be faithful. Read Psalm 25.
What is David asking in this psalm? How does he know God
will answer?

Thinking things through

1. What do you think of the statement, "God always comes
   down"? Do you know such a God? If so, when did you first
   meet this God? If not, how DO you describe the God you
   know in Jesus?
2. Who first introduced you to the God you know? Who has
   been an example and a teacher to you? Who do you need to
   thank for bringing you to Jesus?
3. Have you ever NOT known—or loved—this God? Was there
   ever a time in your life when you were alienated, disappointed,
   or far away from God? What brought you back?
4. Who will be able to help you look at the God you know—
   and your church—with fresh eyes? Do you think you would
   be able to ask them why THEY are Lutherans? Do you think
   you would be able to listen?
5. What is your initial response to the list of five guiding principles? How do you think they may offer a helpful way of artic-
   ulating what it means to be a Lutheran? As you read the
   following chapters, consider how you might rework these
   principles to fit your situation.

Talking it over

*Loving God, you know us better than we dare to know ourselves.
And you know there is never anything we could ever do to deserve
your love. Yet you give it to us freely. Thank you for coming down here
to set us free, at just the right time, when we are lost and broken.
Thank you for Jesus. Amen*

3

Jesus Is Lord

. . . And being found in human form, he humbled himself [came down] and became obedient to the point of death— even death on a cross. Therefore God also highly exalted him and gave him the name that is above every name, so that at the name of Jesus every knee should bend, in heaven and on earth and under the earth, and every tongue should confess that Jesus Christ is Lord, to the glory of God the Father.

⋙ Paul, quoting one of the oldest Christian hymns
Philippians 2:9-11

You proceed from a false assumption: I have no ego to bruise.

⋙ Spock, *Star Trek II: The Wrath of Khan*

While dogma is a set of principles that are believed to be true, a creed is a *formal statement* of those beliefs. In fact, the word *creed* comes from a Latin word (you don't have to memorize this one!) that means, "I believe." As Christians, we have a couple of them. Many of our churches recite the Apostles' Creed every Sunday. Some use the Nicene Creed on special events. And a handful even pull out the lengthy Athanasian Creed to recite once a year on Trinity Sunday. These are the creeds with which most of us are familiar.

But, the truth is, the creeds we are used to using at worship didn't come along until pretty late in the life of the Christian church. The Nicene Creed, for example, wasn't formulated until more than 300 years after Jesus was around. That doesn't mean they're not important. Of course they are. But they weren't the first.

Not long after Jesus was raised from the dead and taken up into heaven, leaving his followers to figure out what to do next, those early Christians formulated their OWN first "guiding principle." They used this "creed" for teaching and preaching; and they used it at baptism. This earliest creed was simply: "Jesus is Lord." All the biblical evidence suggests that this was one of the *first* formal statements of belief. (See Romans 10:9 and 1 Corinthians 12:3.)

And this simple creed, heard on the lips of those ancient Christians, forms the basis for our first guiding principle, too: Jesus Is Lord.

What does this mean?

It sounds simple to say, "Jesus Is Lord." But, I know that for me, it isn't always easy to actually mean it. Most of the time, I want to be the boss of my own life. And I don't think I'm alone. Engraved in the wall at Niketown, right in the middle of the Chicago Loop, are these words: "In our hearts, we are always 12 years old and we are always the quarterback." And it's true. I want to decide which plays to run. I want to call the shots. I want to get all the glory when things go well. I want to be at the center of the huddle. Don't you? Even in our churches, in fact, I sometimes wonder who—or what—is "lord" most of the time.

A few years ago I met a woman who told me about a big mess her congregation had gotten into. It seems the church council had voted to move the grand piano, which sat in the front of the worship space, FIVE INCHES so that they could make room for some new handicap-accessible seating. I'm not sure why the church council was voting on something like this, but there you go. Anyway, the council members agreed on a date and time for meeting at church to move the piano. I'm not sure why they were going to do this themselves, either, but apparently word got out that this was happening.

The appointed time arrived. The church council members gathered in the sanctuary, dressed, I suppose, in appropriate clothing for piano moving and, maybe, feeling a little bit scared—like lightening was going to strike or something if they dared move ANYTHING in such a holy place. But before they even had time to think about it, the director of music burst through the doors of the sanctuary and barreled up the aisle. She said not a word but, rather, communicated her position clearly by hoisting up her generous frame and throwing herself ACROSS THE TOP OF THE PIANO. Presumably she was dressed for piano straddling. At any rate, she flat out, don't-even-try-to-mess-with-me REFUSED to come down off the piano until the church council agreed not to touch it.

Who—or what—was lord in that place, do you think? It is easy to get confused, putting tradition or culture or "my" ideas or whatever, at the center even of our life together as Christians. But I wonder how many of our problems—at church, as well as in our own personal lives—would be solved if we simply remembered that JESUS is Lord, no *thing* and no *one* else.

Fiona is a little friend with a mind of her own. It has always been this way. Even when she was two years old, she wanted to be in charge of everything. In frustration one day, Fiona's mother said, "Fiona, who is the boss of this house?!?" And Fiona, a child of the church if there ever was one, shot back, "Jesus is the boss of this house!"

"Oh yeah," was about all Fiona's mom could think. "That's right."

Most of us were not raised on the planet Vulcan and, unlike Mr. Spock, we do in fact have egos. Big ones. They get in the way at every turn. Sometimes mine will hardly fit through the door. And the only thing that will keep us from self-destructing our homes, our churches, and our lives is remembering that there is only ONE Lord. And his name is Jesus. Everything looks different if we begin here. Because, if we are really serious when we confess that "Jesus Is Lord," then the first and most obvious thing this means is that, therefore, I *can't* be! Neither can you. Or Harvey, the church treasurer. Or Sam, the organist. Or Susan, the pastor. Or Bill, the enthusiastic new member. Or Amelia, the crabby oldest one. The "lord" of my life—and my church—can't be a certain hymnal or a certain building or a certain worship schedule. It can't be the cemetery board or the altar guild. The "lord" can't be whoever has the loudest voice at a meeting. The "lord" can't even be the Bible! Only *Jesus* can be Lord. And that changes everything. Jesus Is Lord. And, first and foremost, that means I can't be.

Not just any Jesus

The very next thing that needs to be said, though, is that the Jesus we're talking about is not just *any* old Jesus. You and I both know that there are a lot of different ways people understand who and what Jesus is. He is a great teacher, a good example, a powerful healer, an important prophet, a wise counselor. And he is, in fact, all those things. But before Jesus is *anything* else, for those of us who are Lutherans, Jesus is the One who meets us at the cross.

Martin Luther referred to what it means to be a *theologian of the cross* in a little document called the *Heidelberg Disputation*, which he presented to a group of scholars in 1518 in Heidelberg, Germany. I wouldn't recommend this essay for light pool side reading this summer, but it's helpful to know that the theology of the cross language contained within it has been pretty important in helping us stay clear, over the centuries, about who and what Jesus is and, for that matter, who and what God is. Brace yourself. Here is what Luther himself said:

18. It is certain that a man must completely despair of his own ability before he is prepared to receive the grace of Christ.

19. That person does not deserve to be called a theologian who looks upon the invisible things of God as though they were clearly perceptible in those things that have actually happened [Romans 1:20].

20. He deserves to be called a theologian, however, who comprehends the visible and manifest things of God seen through suffering and the cross.

21. A theologian of glory calls evil good and good evil. A theologian of the cross calls the thing what it actually is. [6]

In other words, Luther reminds us that, while God could have come to us in all kinds of ways, God chose to come down here to meet us in the most unlikely place of all: On the cross, in the face of an outcast and a stranger, who suffered there and died. And God *had* to do this because we had made such a mess of things.

This is a God that we will never be able to "make sense of." In fact, in some ways, it is impossible to even SEE God on the cross. God's presence there is "invisible." No one in their right mind would imagine that God, the maker of everything that is, seen and unseen, would come down here to us in such an odd and sad and scary way. No one can really understand this. And, as soon as we think we have God all figured out, we are as far away from God as we can possibly be. To say that Jesus is Lord, the One we see on the cross, is to acknowledge that we will always be just a little off balance in this relationship. We will always need to be prepared to be surprised.

---

[6] Martin Luther, *Heidelberg Disputation*, 1518, in *Martin Luther's Basic Theological Writings*, ed. Timothy F. Lull (Minneapolis: Fortress Press, 1989), p. 31.

In fact, I'd like to suggest that if we really believe Jesus is Lord —*this* Jesus, the One who dies on the cross for us—then we will have to be ready for anything . . . and honest about everything.

Ready for anything

If Jesus really is Lord, then we will find ourselves surprised again and again by the God who meets us. This was certainly the experience of those who got to know Jesus first hand. The disciples were surprised one day to find Jesus calmly having a conversation with a woman who was everything they had been taught to despise and distrust; she was from a different religion, a foreign land, and her morals left more than a little to be desired (John 4). The Pharisees were surprised —and a bit horrified— to stumble across Jesus sharing a meal with Matthew and Matthew's rough-and-tumble friends, guys who ripped people off for a living and spent their lives lurking about on the edges of decent society (Matthew 9). Peter was downright stunned to hear the Holy Spirit speaking through Cornelius, a soldier who loved God but just wasn't welcome in the holy places Peter was used to visiting (Acts 10). God will meet us, Jesus said, in the most unexpected places, in the hungry and the sick and those in prison (Matthew 18:38-40). Jesus' friends were always being knocked for a loop.

Jesus' friends still get knocked for a loop every once in a while. A few years ago, near the end of the strangest presidential election in American history, I was driving along in the back of a taxicab, listening to a news report about the latest court decision. I was feeling a little dismayed, like a lot of Americans I guess, that the whole thing was taking so long and seemed to be so convoluted. But my driver was from Turkey.

"You Americans just don't realize how fortunate you are," he said, startling me out of my cynical funk. "I come from a place where we have seen blood run in the streets. Here, you settle things peacefully."

Even in a post–9/11 world, his words carry the weight of truth. They convict me every time I start feeling complacent about the blessings I have been given . . . or lazy about my responsibilities toward the rest of the people on the planet. In the voice of a stranger, I heard a word from God.

Some friends of mine had the same experience one summer when they gave their vacation time to spend it working at a children's shelter in the poorest neighborhood in San Miguel, Mexico. They spent their days at Casa de los Angeles cleaning, cooking, and caring for the infants and children who are sheltered there during the day so that their parents can work. These adults came back telling stories about the impact this experience had on them. "Spend a week living among the poor in Mexico, walking in their streets, shopping in their markets, caring for their children, working hand-in-hand," one of the team members wrote, "and if your heart does not ache for them, you are living with your eyes closed. I know mine were before I came here."

Because Jesus is Lord, we can expect to be surprised by a God who comes to us in the most unlooked-for ways and in the most unexpected places. We can expect, even, to be *wrong* sometimes. As Lutherans, we readily admit that there is just no way we are ever going to be able to get our arms all the way around this God thing. There is *nothing* expected about the God who meets us in the One who hangs there upon the cross.

This is one of the reasons Lutherans are reluctant to make definitive and irreversible statements about what is unerringly "true" or unquestionably "right." We are more comfortable with paradoxes. We believe, for example, that God's people in Christ are both "saint" and "sinner" all at the same time. We don't mind living with a little "gray" when it comes to hard issues and tough choices. We are careful about not jumping to conclusions, and when we say, "Here I Stand," you can be certain we have thought and prayed long and hard about it.

Because the God we know in Jesus is the One who comes to us on the cross, we know that as soon as we think we have it all together, with all our I's dotted and all our T's crossed, we have it as wrong as wrong can be. As soon as we think we have figured out *exactly* who we are and who God is and what our worship should look like and what kind of people are acceptable in God's house and how our churches should function and where the PIANO is supposed to sit, we have wandered as far away from God as we can go.

This is also why you shouldn't often find Lutherans slinging Scripture at each other in an argument. It isn't that the Bible doesn't matter. It does. But the Bible only makes sense when it is read through the cross. The cross is like a lens that makes everything, even the Bible, look different. And, when seen through the cross, the Bible is—before it is anything else—the story of a God who always comes down, full of surprises, to set us free. I can't pull a couple of verses out of the Bible and piece them together to make my "argument," whatever that might be. When stripped away from the cross, the words in the Bible are just that: words. Even Scripture must bow to the surprising God who meets us on the cross.

Honest about everything

Frankly, though, the most surprising thing of all is that the One who meets us on the cross came for ME. If "Jesus Is Lord" means, first of all, that I can't be, it also means that *I don't have to be, either.* And, for that, we should all be very thankful.

Frankly, I wouldn't make a very good god. None of us would. That's why the story of the invisible man is really the story of every man . . . and woman. The H. G. Wells story *The Invisible Man* was remade into the film *Hollow Man* a few years ago.

In the film, a scientist (played by Kevin Bacon) becomes invisible in a laboratory accident and discovers that, in fact, "it's amazing what you can do when you don't have to look at yourself in the mirror anymore." Bacon's invisible character starts out by playing practical jokes on his unsuspecting and unappreciative friends. The story ends with rape and murder, and the man who is invisible on the outside also ends up being rotten on the inside. You knew things were going nowhere good right from the start, though, when Bacon is warned by another scientist, "You are messing with the laws of nature. You will be punished." To which Bacon, wearing an appropriately evil smirk, responds, "Frank, how many times have I told you: I *am* God."

This movie might have been panned by the critics, but there were more than a few moments when it made my skin crawl. It hit just a little too close to home. The truth is, I am too often tempted to walk around thinking I am God, too . . . or ought to be. And, hey, I know I'm not the only one. This is the *original* sin, after all.

The serpent snuck into the garden and tickled the woman's ear: "Hey, there, little lady . . . word on the street is that you're not supposed to eat from that tree over there . . . yeah, you know, that beautiful one standing in the middle of the garden. Want to know a secret? If you eat from THAT one, you'll know as much as God." So the first thing she and her mate did was to stride right over and take a bite. That, by the way, was right before they got marched out of paradise.

Over and over again, this is what we do. We try to *be* God. No wonder we spend so much of our lives in trouble. The truth is, we make terrible gods. And, so, when we say we believe that Jesus is Lord, if we're thinking at all clearly, we will breathe a deep sigh of relief. If Jesus is Lord, not only does this mean I can't be, it means I don't *have* to be, either.

This Jesus, who came down in the form of stranger and an outcast, came to meet us right here in the middle of our sinfulness and shame. This Jesus convicts us with the power of his

> If Jesus is Lord, then I can't be . . . and, thank you, God, I don't HAVE to be, either.

love and makes us look at ourselves more honestly than we would ever dare to do or even want to do on our own. In his cross, we see our own failures . . . our own fault. And we know the truth that Jesus came to be our Savior because we needed to be saved. We needed to be set free from our own stupidity, our self-centeredness, and our insistence on making our own way in the world. Like Paul, I know what God wants me to do, but I *cannot do it*. And the things I don't want to do, I do anyway. Wretch that I am! Who will rescue me from this body of death? Thanks be to God through Jesus Christ our Lord (Romans 7).

In this Jesus, we meet a God who loves us not because of everything we have done to deserve it but, SURPRISE, in spite of everything we have ever done to push God away, in spite of every time we have demanded the right to worship gods of our own making, in spite of it all. In *this* Jesus we see ourselves clearly . . . and we see God, a God of surprising grace who has given everything there is to give so that we can be set free.

Do this in remembrance of me

Remembering that Jesus is Lord takes work because it is just so incredibly hard to remember that we are not. That's why I loved the picture of Tiger Woods, four days after winning the U.S. Open by 15 strokes at Pebble Beach a few years ago. He was caddying for his former college roommate, Jerry Chang, who was attempting to qualify for the U.S. Public Links Championship, an amateur tournament. Tiger was out on the course with Jerry at 6 A.M. and stayed with him for two rounds in 100-degree Nevada heat. Jerry didn't even qualify. But Tiger was out there, carrying his clubs, remembering, I imagine, who he is. And, perhaps, remembering who he ISN'T.

As Lutherans, we remember who we are—and who we are not—every time Jesus meets us in the Word and in the Sacraments. In fact, as a church, we are *defined* by these two things. In the Augsburg Confession, which for almost 500 years has helped shape our understanding of what it means to be Lutheran, the church is described as "the assembly of all believers among whom the gospel is purely preached and the holy sacraments are administered according to the gospel." [7] As the church, we gather for worship and turn our hearts to hear God speak to us in the Word. We come forward, sometimes on our knees, with outstretched hands to receive the presence of Christ in bread and wine. We remember every single day, if we follow Luther's advice, the baptism that first showered God's love and grace upon our lives. There is nothing we need to do or could do to deserve these gifts. They are freely offered at the hand of a loving God. Because we haven't earned them, they remind us again and again that Jesus—*only* Jesus—is Lord. Right at the center of our life together, in other words, is an encounter with a surprising God who always comes down to set us free. "Do this in remembrance of me," Jesus said. And we do.

Letting Jesus be Lord of our lives—and of our congregations— means making sure that no *thing* and no *one* else is allowed to be.

---

[7] *The Augsburg Confession—German Text—Article VII, Concerning the Church, The Book of Concord: The Confessions of the Evangelical Lutheran Church*, eds. Robert Kolb and Timothy J. Wengert (Minneapolis: Fortress Press, 2000), p. 42.

This is sometimes easier said than done. Maybe that is why the apostle Paul had to be so clear and so hard about it. He went to a lot of trouble to remind his friends that there could be no boasting among those who confess that Jesus is Lord. (Check out Romans 3 and 1 Corinthians 1.) Over and over again he scolded them for forgetting that, without Jesus, they were nothing. And he is ruthlessly honest about his own life. He told his own sorry story over and over again, about how once he was lost but was found only by the grace of God. He never wanted anyone—including himself—to forget that it is all about the surprising God we know in Jesus. "I have been crucified with Christ," he wrote, "and it is no longer I who live, but it is Christ who lives in me" (Galatians 2:20). Can you hear in his words the same desperate prayer I hear? "Please, Lord Jesus, help me die to myself so that you and you alone can live in me. Set me free from everything that isn't You! Help me remember who I am, so that I can remember who you are."

Only Jesus is Lord.

Wrestling with the Word

1. The prophet Isaiah was speaking to the people of Israel as they sat on the brink of political, economic, religious, and cultural disaster. God used Isaiah to try and turn these people around before it was too late. It didn't work. But it might have if they had just listened. Read Isaiah 1:1-4, 16-20. What was it Isaiah said they were doing so wrong? And what was it they needed to do differently?

2. The disciples were often getting things mixed up. Read Matthew 18:1-4. What crazy question did they ask Jesus here in this passage? And what was his answer? What is challenging about Jesus' answer? What is freeing?

Thinking things through

1. Everybody has things in their life that could easily become "gods," turning their hearts away from the ONE God. What are the things on your list? What idolatry do you need to confess?

2. How is it going in your church? What things too often become "lord" in your congregation? If you're not sure how to answer this question, ask yourself: "What could we CHANGE around here that would make people mad, even if we did it for a really good reason?"

3. Where is the most surprising place you have ever heard God's voice? What did you hear God say?

4. If you—and your church—were to really confess "Jesus Is Lord!" and mean it, what are some of the things you might have to give up . . . or take on . . . or do differently? How does this make you feel? Do you think you're up to it?

Talking it over

Forgive us, gracious God, for so often forgetting that YOU are Lord. Forgive us for putting ourselves and the things of this world ahead of you. Forgive us for our arrogance and our idolatry and our stubborn pride. Have mercy on us. Make us open to your surprising presence in our lives. And, come. Come and be our king. Amen

4

Everyone Is Welcome

For by grace you have been saved through faith, and this is not your own doing; it is the gift of God—not the result of works, so that no one may boast.

⋙ Ephesians 2:8-9

We need even more reasons to love [Jesus] in this millennium. We've got to love him for his boldness. Jesus is my license to be bold.

⋙ Sheron C. Patterson, womanist theologian and pastor
New Faith, by Sheron C. Patterson, Fortress Press, 2000

I like running just a little bit faster than the average guy.

⋙ Richard Petty, race car driver
Quotable Petty, by Charles Chandler, Towle House Publishing, 2002

Guiding Principle #2 for those of us who are God's people, through Jesus . . . who also happen to be Lutheran . . . has to be this: Everyone Is Welcome. And this, friends, is where things really get moving. That's how it is when we move over and recognize that God is at the wheel. When Jesus is really and truly Lord, unexpected things start to happen. And they happen faster, sometimes, than we are ready for them.

My favorite Gospel is the one with Mark's name attached to it. It was the earliest of the four Gospels. It was written closest to the ground, nearest to Jesus' life, and it has an urgency about it you just don't find in the other three. According to Mark's Gospel, Jesus was IMMEDIATELY driven out into the wilderness after his baptism; the disciples IMMEDIATELY dropped

51

everything and followed Jesus when he called; the leper was
IMMEDIATELY healed just because Jesus said a word. And
that's all just in the first chapter. You can hardly catch your breath
as you read Mark's version of things.

The book of Acts is a little bit like that, too. You just never
know what's going to happen next as you read it. The disciples,
living in the middle of it, didn't know, either. They are all gathered
in one place when SUDDENLY the heavens burst open and
God's Spirit was poured out upon them, ready or not (Acts 2).
Paul was traveling merrily on his way to Damascus, where he was
scheduled to arrest some Christians and have them killed, never
even thinking he was doing anything other than his Father's business, when SUDDENLY Jesus appeared to him and changed his
plans forever (Acts 9). Peter was in prison, probably thinking his
days were numbered, when SUDDENLY an angel of the Lord
showed up and led him on a daring escape that ensured he would
live to preach another day (Acts 12).

When you confess with your lips and believe in your heart that
"Jesus is Lord," you better be ready for anything.

Are you?

No lines, ever

Here is the flat-out truth about Guiding Principle #2.
Jesus, the Lord, welcomed everybody, especially the foreigner,
the excluded, the sad and lonely and hurting. In fact, that got
him in trouble with the religious leaders of his day more than
almost anything else. So, if Jesus loved and welcomed someone,
then who am I to say I'm not going to do that?

The truth is, none of us deserves to be welcomed or loved by
Jesus. Anyone who has spent a while looking into the face of the
God who meets us on the cross, knows that. We know that we
have been saved by grace through faith alone and not because of
anything we have ever done to earn or deserve it. We know that

we are right with God only because, in an astonishing act of grace, God came down here to meet us. God didn't draw a line and say, "I'm coming for you and you and you. But you, over there, you're out of luck." And if God didn't draw a line, why do we think we somehow have the right to draw one?

I first found myself on the "other" side of that line for the first time when I was about 10. I was old enough to have had a lot of little crushes before, even to have had a first boyfriend. Bobby and I were in first grade when we exchanged bubble-gum machine rings. But that was just puppy love. With Billy, though, it was the real thing. I was just turning around from the cafeteria window one day, carrying my tray of soggy vegetables and mystery meat, when Billy ran up from behind me and planted a kiss on the side of my head, right in front of the whole fifth grade. It was a little awkward. But it was my FIRST kiss and it made my legs go all wobbly. It gave my best friend, Carol, and me something to talk about for days. I knew then that what Billy and I had was something special.

It was Billy's mom who wrecked it. Carol's mom had picked the three of us up after school one day. Carol's mom was driving and Billy's mom, Mrs. M., who had come along for the ride, was sitting in the passenger seat beside her. I could hear them talking about us. I heard my name a few times, but I really wasn't paying much attention to their conversation because I was in the back seat sitting right between my best friend and my boyfriend. Now, Billy wasn't exactly holding my hand back there, but his hand was just close enough to mine that they would sort of brush up against each other every once in a while and we were careful not to move them away. I was about as happy as a 10-year-old can be. But our giggling conversation came screeching to an end when we heard Billy's mom loudly say, "What do you MEAN she's a Catholic?" Carol's mom didn't say another word. We didn't dare say anything either. We all just waited for whatever was going to happen next. And that's when Billy's mom turned around and looked at her son, ignoring the scared little girl sitting next to him, and said, "I don't ever want you to see this fish-eating Catholic again."

I felt Billy's hand move slowly away. And we rode the rest of the way to my house in silence. When I got home, I went into my room and closed my door and cried.

Mrs. M. was a Methodist, I think. But that's not why she said what she said. In fact, *I don't know why* she said it. Maybe she just grew up in a time when these kinds of prejudices were common on BOTH sides of the fence, and she never knew any other way of looking at things. Maybe she had some reason to be angry with a particular Catholic and she was taking it out on all of us. Or maybe she underestimated the damage her words would do because she figured we were "just kids" and therefore harder, somehow, to wound. Or maybe she didn't want her 10-year-old son holding hands with ANYBODY, and this was the quickest way she could think of to stop it. Or maybe she was just mean.

I don't know why Mrs. M. said what she said that day. But I DO know—and I even knew then—that what she said was wrong. And it was wrong, NOT just because it hurt my feelings . . . or because I say so. It was wrong because GOD says so.

The ONLY people, remember, that Jesus ever lost his temper with were the people who went around drawing the lines. "Woe to you, scribes and Pharisees, hypocrites!" Jesus yelled. *"For you lock people out of the kingdom of heaven"* (Matthew 23:13). Jesus, on the other hand, threw the gates of heaven open to anyone who would enter. "Those who are well have no need of a physician," he said, "but those who are sick" (Luke 5:31). Jesus came for those who needed him the most. And he welcomed them with open arms. It didn't matter what you did for a living, or what country you were born in, or even whether you were a man or woman. It didn't matter how messed up you had let your life become. In fact, the worse off you were, the bigger the welcome. "There will be more joy in heaven," Jesus said, "over one sinner who repents than over ninety-nine righteous persons!" (Luke 15:7). And Jesus warned everybody else to back off when it comes to standing in judgment of these people. "Do not judge, and you will not be judged; do not condemn, and you will not be condemned" (Luke 6:37). Better yet, Jesus said, and more to the point: Take the log out of your own eye before you start trying to take the speck out of anybody else's!

This was Jesus' way of reminding all of us, as if we could forget, that our relationship with him starts at the foot of the cross . . . where NO ONE has anything to boast about. Standing there, at the cross, I don't even dare look around to see who else is standing there, too. I'm too embarrassed. I know that everybody there would see me the way I really am, sinful and weak, standing in the need of prayer. But if I DID dare to look around, I would see a whole bunch of people who look just like me. "Come to me, all you that are weary and are carrying heavy burdens," Jesus said (Matthew 11:28). And here we all are.

As long as Jesus is Lord, there can be NO lines. Not because it would be *mean* if we didn't welcome everyone. Not because I say so. But because the God we know in Jesus says so. And Jesus is Lord.

Some more Latin

Frankly, if we ever DO start drawing lines at my church, I'm in big trouble. And our old friend, Martin, would have been, too. Luther was a remarkable man. In fact, as we counted down to the year 2000, Luther made it to the top of several lists of the millennium's most important people. He led the Reformation 500 years ago that helped the Christian church rediscover the wonders of God's startling grace. He unchained the Bible, translating it into a language ordinary people could understand.

He opened up the worship experience to everyone, insisting that people be able to sing and pray in their own language, and he made sure everyone had access to both the bread and wine of Holy Communion. He set people free from superstitious ideas about how to get to heaven and introduced them to the God who always comes down. He put the highest possible priority on educating everyone, even children, in the basic truths of the faith. He reminded the church that it was more than a pastor's club and that, in fact, every Christian is a minister. In fact, he encouraged pastors to *get* married so they could experience the holiness of everyday life.

Luther's courage and clarity changed the world. But he was far from perfect. He had a terrible temper and a pretty foul mouth. He called supporters of the Pope "papal asses," and worse. He ate too much and probably sometimes drank too much, too. He said some pretty terrible things, even for medieval times, about women. He wrestled with depression; often falling into spiritual funks from which his friends worried he might not recover. Sometimes he said one thing, and then did another. The horrible things he wrote five centuries ago about the Jews were used, in this century, to justify the most outrageous and unforgivable actions taken during World War II. Of course, Luther could not have foreseen that his words would be used in such a destructive way, but that he said such things at all reveals his fiery and combative nature.

And, I'll say it again, if we started drawing lines to let some people in and keep others out, I would be hard pressed to know which side Luther would be on. It would be a little embarrassing, wouldn't it; to build a church our namesake wouldn't be allowed to join? So, let's not.

Anyway, as Lutherans, we don't have to. We believe that, as God's people, we have been set free, through Jesus, from sin and death and all the other rotten stuff that messes up our lives.

But we do NOT believe that means the struggle is over. We know that we are *simul justus et peccator*. This is another Latin phrase worth knowing, because it came out of the Reformation 500 years ago and is as helpful today as it was then. It means, simply, that we are *simultaneously saint and sinner*. We are AT THE SAME TIME both holy and all messed up. We have been set free from sin and are up to our ears in it all in the same moment. We are saved; and we need, every single day, to be washed again in the waters of baptism and set free all over again.

This concept is the only way we can make sense of the real stories of all those people in the Bible who were, in fact, God's faithful people, but who at the same time managed to make a big mess of everything. The great King David, for example, who couldn't keep his pants on. And Jonah, who folded when things got too rough and didn't go back to work until a whale swallowed him and spit him up onto a new shore. There is something deeply TRUE about this uniquely Lutheran concept. It isn't as easy as saying that, because I'm saved, everything is beautiful and life is perfect. It just isn't. The truth is, life is more complicated than that, even life with God.

A motley crew

We are a motley crew, we Christians. We are so amazingly holy. We do so many remarkable and courageous things. And at the same time we are, every single one of us, such a mess. We are just as likely to run as we are to stand, to lie as we are to tell the truth, to gossip as we are to give. We too often say one thing and do another. And, God help us if anyone has been writing down everything we've ever said in order to use it 500 years later.

I woke up one morning to a singer called Pink on my clock radio telling my life story in her song "Don't Let Me Get Me," singing, "I'm a hazard to myself." It almost made me want to run out to pick up her album *Missundaztood*. There was no misunderstanding the message here. Too often, we ARE our own worst enemies. We are careless and selfish, and who would want us?!?

Well, Jesus does, because Jesus loves sinners. And that makes all the difference. Jesus opens his arms up wide, upon that cross, and he welcomes us all; every single *simul justus et peccator* one of us. If we are "in" here, it isn't because we deserve to be at all. It's because Jesus made it possible. Paul knew this. That's why he challenged his friends in Rome to "welcome one another . . . just as Christ has welcomed you" (Romans 15:7). In fact, those who knew Jesus in biblical times *all* knew that they were there, beside him, only by the grace of God.

"Hey, Peter," I can imagine Jesus saying as they sat with their friends around a campfire late one night, "remember the look on your face when I told you to come follow me?" YEAH! YOU TOLD ME I'D BE FISHING FOR PEOPLE! I THOUGHT YOU WERE CRAZY!

"Oh, yeah, and remember when that big storm kicked up," somebody else would say, "and we were all out in the middle of the lake. Jesus was so calm about it all . . . but Philip just about wet his pants!"

The man they met in Jerusalem would be there, the one who couldn't walk, who used to make his living as a beggar. "I remember how scared I was when Jesus told me to get up and walk," he would say.

"YEAH," said Thomas. "BUT NOT AS SCARED AS THOSE PHARISEES WERE WHEN THEY SAW YOU DO IT!"

They would all tell their stories. The man who made his living as a soldier, doing all the kinds of terrible things soldiers are sometimes called upon to do, whose beautiful young daughter Jesus brought back to life. Zacchaeus, the little miser, whom Jesus coaxed down out of a tree. Matthew, and all of his tax-collecting buddies, to whose house Jesus invited himself over for dinner. And, of course, there would be that woman, the one who was very nearly put to death for adultery until, at the last moment, Jesus stepped in. "I'll never forget the sound of those clattering stones," she would whisper, "as those men all walked away."

Every single one of the people who followed Jesus, back in the day, knew exactly why they were there. It wasn't because they were better than anybody else. It wasn't because they were smarter or more faithful or more well behaved. It was only this: Jesus had welcomed them, with open arms, just as they were.

Look up for a minute, and into the eyes of the One you see on the cross. I dare you to see what he sees when he looks at you. You know this, don't you? We are saved by God's grace, as a gift, through our *faith* in the One who came down here to set us free and not because of a single thing that we have ever done or said or thought to earn it. We are here because of God's unconditional love in Jesus Christ.

Just who in the world do we think we are, anyway, thinking that it's our job to keep somebody else out?

By the way

I don't know what happened to Mrs. M. I never saw her again after that day. But the last time I saw Billy was about 10 years ago. He was working for Greenpeace, saving the whales and the rain forests. He had like three holes pierced in each ear and a ring in his nose. And I'm thinking that if the friends he brought home to meet mom looked ANYTHING like him, then Mrs. M. has had to do some real stretching and some real growing over the years. I hope so.

Wrestling with the Word

1. Jesus didn't have much patience for those who insisted on drawing lines that would lump some people into a holy

category and some people somewhere else. He told a story to his friends to make this point. Read Luke 18:9-14. What was it that really made Jesus mad in this story? Do you identify with either of these characters? Maybe you can identify with both of them.

2. Paul's friends in Corinth were arguing about who among them was the best. Maybe they were even trying to figure out what the qualifications were for being part of their church. Paul writes to them to help them work this out. Read 1 Corinthians 1:26-31. What does he say to them? How do you think it made them feel? What, if anything, do you think they did differently as a result of what Paul said?

Thinking things through

1. Do you ever feel like God is taking you places you are not ready to go? Do you feel that way, now?
2. Have you ever been made to feel unwelcome? What happened?
3. Is it hard for you to think about the disciples and other people in the Bible as anything other than "saints"? If you see them as real people, with flaws like ours, how does this change the way you think about yourself—or your church?
4. How welcoming is your church? Can you think of anyone who would NOT be welcome there? What do you think about that? What do you think Jesus would think about that?

Talking it over

We give you thanks, O Lord, for your overflowing love! How do you put up with us?!? For welcoming us when we had wandered far away from you, we thank and praise you. For showering us with forgiveness when we had turned our backs on you, we thank and praise you. For saving us, again and again, from our own stupidity and selfishness, we thank and praise you. Help us welcome one another the way you have welcomed us. In Jesus' name. Amen

5

Love Changes People

But you are a chosen race, a royal priesthood, a holy nation, God's own people, in order that you may proclaim the mighty acts of him who called you out of darkness and into his marvelous light.

⊷ Peter, reminding people why Jesus bothered
   1 Peter 2:9

If a kid asks where rain comes from, I think a cute thing to tell him is "God is crying." And if he asks why God is crying, another cute thing to tell him is "Probably because of something you did.

⊷ Jack Handey, *Deep Thoughts*, Berkeley Publishing Group, 1992

Is it just me, or is the world getting meaner? No, I'm serious. Now, I am NOT that old. But I can remember going downtown with my mom and, while she was shopping in Goldblatt's, I was riding the gold plated elevator. You know, the kind with the gate in front of it. A distinguished gentleman, wearing a hat and white gloves and brass buttons on his colorful suit coat, ran the elevator. "Going up, miss?" he would politely say. He didn't even mind when I went up . . . and then down . . . and then up again . . . all afternoon. But just try to get on—or OFF—an elevator today. Didn't anyone ever tell these people that you're supposed to let the people on the elevator get off *before* you try to cram through the doors?!?

Surveys tell us that Americans believe that only 38% of people can be trusted. And more than half of all 18- to 29-year-olds believe that other people will take advantage of them if they have half a chance.[8]

There is a mean-spiritedness in our culture that has been softened a little, perhaps, by the World Trade Center attack. For now, anyway, people seem to be trying to be a bit gentler with one another. But, as one New Yorker told me, they'll know things are getting back to normal when people start honking at each other on the streets again and shaking their fists using interesting gestures that only other New Yorkers would understand. It's almost like mean is normal.

And, forgive me for saying this, but I sometimes think I see this mean-spiritedness reflected in some corners of the Christian church. Do you see it, too?

LOVE changes people

It was 10:30 on Friday night, and I was looking for the highway that was supposed to take me 40 miles north from the airport in Charlotte, North Carolina, to a conference I was attending the next day in Salisbury, when I came to a fork in the road. Before me I was faced with a choice between I-85 North and I-77 East. And, there on my right, loomed this gigantic billboard. Flames of fire shot up along the bottom of the sign and its message could not have been clearer.

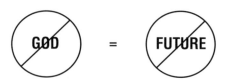

Apparently, there are some Christians who think this approach —just scare the heck out of people—actually works. In a bathroom stall in a MacDonald's restaurant, just outside of Rennsalaer,

---

[8] Susan Mitchell, *American Attitudes*, Ithaca, N.Y.: New Strategist, 2000.

Indiana, on another Friday afternoon, I saw all the usual goofy graffiti you see in such places. Lennie Loves Maggie. Bob & Sue Forever. POOLS RULE. (OK, I guess I *don't* know what that means!) Then, this message: "Jesus is coming back soon. Will you be ready???"

God bless them, I think they mean well. But somebody ought to tell these folks that it is God's *love* that makes the difference for people. Not the law. Not a list of rules you better follow or else. Not whacking people upside the head with a Bible. Notice that when Peter blessed his friends, rejoicing with them that they had become "a holy nation, God's own people," he reminded them that this was all because they had been *chosen* and called. They had been *loved* into it (1 Peter 2:9). He doesn't mention anything about being whacked upside the head.

Now, I have a teenager at home, and a 10-year-old. I love them more than I can say. I would never actually whack them, not even with a Bible. But, I confess, it is sometimes easier to say: "Just do this because the Bible says! Just BE this because the Bible says!" And as soon as the words slip out from between my lips, I wish I could grab them and shove them all back in. I regret every syllable.

The law, Paul says, IS important. I don't mean to suggest it isn't. God's law is like a "disciplinarian" who helps us clearly see that without Jesus we are lost (Galatians 3). Looking up at that towering list of God's rules and realizing how impossible it would be for us to ever fulfill them, reminds us that there really *isn't* anything we could ever do to turn that arrow around and make our way up to God.

But people aren't really *changed* by rulebooks or lectures or laws. You know that. Can YOU honestly say that your life is different because somebody beat you over the head with a Bible or scared you half to death? An experience like this might make you get up and go to church for a few weeks in a row, or even months or years. But what really changes people over the long run, what makes people different, what moves people surely and steadily along the path of faith and holiness and hope, what made all the difference in *my* life. . . is LOVE, the love of God through Jesus Christ.

I wish, frankly, that our churches did a better job of this. Even for those of us who know better, it really is just too easy to scare people away. Sometimes we do that even when we don't mean to.

A young woman I know, for example, grew up as a member of a little Lutheran church somewhere in rural North Dakota. The church was built back in 1913, and it is closed now. Even when my friend was little, back in the 1970s, the membership of the church was dying off. There weren't many children at all . . . in fact, she was the only kid in her first communion and confirmation class. You can imagine, can't you, with only grown ups around, and most of them elderly, what a SERIOUS place this church seemed to her to be. The worst thing about it all for her, though, was that the church didn't have a septic system. So, way down in the musty, creaky, spooky basement, the church elders had installed the next best thing: A high tech, environmentally safe, FIRE toilet! From the outside, a fire toilet looks like any ordinary toilet. But *inside* it is specially designed to burn up whatever has happened to fall in as soon as the lid is closed. The fire toilet made a loud whooshing sound every time it went to work. And it smelled like sulfur. That poor little girl was absolutely certain that there, in the basement of her church, she was looking right into the mouth of hell. She was five years old. And it scared the daylights out of her.

Sometimes, the way the church—OUR church—has done things has scared people away before they even had a chance to meet the One welcomes them in. We haven't always meant that to be the case. But that's what has happened, usually on accident—

and sometimes, maybe, on purpose—because of something we've said or done, or something we've failed to do.

This is why Guiding Principle #3 is so important: Love Changes People. It keeps right up in front of us, right before our very eyes, the challenge to carry out in our lives—and in our churches—what we know to be true in our hearts. Without apology, in rather radical fashion, we declare the OPPOSITE of what everything in our legalistic, take-no-prisoners culture tells us is true. *We have been met by the Lord Jesus, who has welcomed us with open arms.* And we declare that it has been his welcome—and his LOVE!—which has made everything new.

In other words, as God's people through Jesus, who also happen to be Lutheran, if we have to pick a foot to lead with—love or law—we will pick love, every time. Every single time I start thinking that maybe this is the WRONG foot, I think about Scott. Scott came to Cross of Glory when he was in third grade. He and his little sister had never been baptized. His dad was raised in a Jewish home and his mom had never really had any church background at all. We got the kids baptized and then Scott joined our First Communion program. At Cross of Glory, this is a family affair. So many of our members haven't had a church background that First Communion is a good time to teach *everybody* what this Meal is all about.

So Scott and his parents came to all the classes together and worshiped together, as a part of the program, during Holy Week. A few days before First Communion Sunday, Scott's dad came to talk to me. He said that, even though he had chosen not to be baptized with his kids—his parents were still alive and his dad had been sick and, besides, he just wasn't sure he was ready—he had been listening closely during those First Communion classes. And he was wondering if it would be OK for him to take communion with his son that Sunday.

Now, you know the rule, right? You're supposed to be *baptized before* you take communion. And I was thinking about that rule as I spent the longest nine seconds of my life looking into Ron's eyes. Finally, I said, "Ron, Jesus ate with all kinds of people while he was here on earth. He ate with tax collectors and prostitutes. And I know he ate with a whole lot of Jewish people. I think he would LOVE to eat with you." That Sunday, as I gave communion to Scott and his family, I felt like Jesus was there, smiling over Ron's shoulder.

A year later, at about the same time of year, Ron and I had coffee. "You know that song the band sang during Holy Week last week," he said, "the one about Peter and how he denied Jesus and Jesus forgave him?"

"Yes," I said. "I remember."

"During that song," Ron said, "I knew for the first time that Jesus really is the Messiah."

Ron was baptized not long after that. He had his head bowed over the font so he couldn't see the tears in my eyes. But they were there. They were there a few months ago, too, when Ron's son Scott became the newest member of our preaching team. He is a senior in high school and a remarkable young man. He preached a powerful sermon his first time out about how being part of a community that loves him unconditionally has changed his life. Every ounce
of confidence and courage and self-worth he has today, Scott said, has been a gift to him from a community that believes in a God who always comes down.

And I am thankful that he won't let me forget it.

Love CHANGES people

It all begins with love. But, not for a moment do I think we should underestimate just how powerful that love can be. Love really does *change* everything.

I don't know why, but I think it is at least a little strange that I learned so much about what a powerful force love is from a former Marine. He had been in the Marine Corps for 16 years and, the last I heard, was a pastor of a Lutheran church somewhere in the Deep South. He still looks like a Marine—shiny shoes, a straight back. Don't even ask me how this conversation started, but before I knew it he was explaining to me the meaning of *semper fi*. Yes, this is another Latin phrase; no, you do not have to memorize it. But it is important to know that *semper fi* means "always faithful." My new friend explained that, for a Marine, this loyalty extends beyond just loyalty to country. Marines are loyal to one another. The whole deal is built on trust. Marines need to know that they can count on each other 100%. In fact, they are instructed that if they get injured in combat, they are to "fall forward." That way the troops behind them won't get tripped up on their bodies as they are dying. This trust, my friend said, this absolute loyalty to one another, this environment of security and confidence, "makes it possible for people to do what they could never do otherwise."

Yes, indeed. The Bible is full of stories about people whose lives were transformed when the God who loves them met them where and as they were. These people found themselves, as a result of this meeting, doing things they never imagined were even possible. For example, when Jesus called little Zacchaeus down out of the tree in Luke 19, the man had every reason to expect a scolding. "You have cheated people out of their money, Zacchaeus," Jesus could have said. "You have lied and taken advantage of people in need." Jesus could have thrown the book at him. Or whacked him with it. He could have threatened or embarrassed him, or spelled out the eternal consequences of his behavior. He could have drawn a little picture in the sand, laying out in no uncertain terms the unhappy future, which lie ahead of him if God wasn't in it. But Jesus didn't do any of those things.

Jesus said, "Hey Zacchaeus, are you hungry? Let's go get something to eat." And Zacchaeus, overwhelmed by such a surprising welcome, gave Jesus his heart. "I'm going to fix *everything* I've ever done wrong," Zacchaeus shouted. "Nothing is ever going to be the same!"

Nothing IS the same once you have been touched by the boundless love of Jesus. Martin Luther introduced his little treatise on *Christian Liberty* by talking about the result of his own encounter with this loving God. Anyone, he said, "who has had even a faint taste of it can never write, speak, meditate, or hear enough concerning it. It is a living 'spring of water welling up to eternal life.' " [9] No one can dispute how radically *his* life changed once he met the God who set him free. God's love gives us confidence and courage and inspiration to do things we would never do otherwise.

I don't care who you are, something *happens* when you meet the God who loves you and welcomes you home. Not everybody decides, on the spot, like Zacchaeus, to give away half of what they own and pay back every debt and make up with everyone they've ever cheated. Not everybody marches out to lead a Reformation that will change the world. But SOMETHING happens.

The apostle Paul, who spent most of his letters clarifying and re-clarifying the priority of grace and hammering home the message that it is LOVE that sets us free, ended nearly every one of those letters with a call to "lead a life worthy of God!" That is what he set out to do, after his little meeting with Jesus. If ever anybody deserved a good clobbering, it was Paul, who was going

---

[9] Martin Luther, "A Treatise On Christian Liberty," trans. W. A. Lambert, revised by Harold J. Grimm, as found in *Martin Luther's Basic Theological Writings*, ed. Timothy F. Lull (Minneapolis: Fortress Press, 1989), p. 595.

around the countryside killing Christians. Instead, Jesus put Paul to work, setting people free all over the place through the love of God; and planting churches through which the good news about this God could be shared.

Those of us who stand on grace need to be very careful not to give the idea that life in Jesus is all mushy and lazy and easy, just because it is centered and grounded in love. No way. This is hard work. In fact, when Luther traveled the countryside in those days following the Reformation and discovered how many lazy, mushy Christians there were, he was beside himself. He went home and wrote a couple of very important books that would be used for the next five centuries to teach the faith because, frankly, no one back then was bothering to learn it. That's where the Large and the Small Catechism came from. The Small Catechism was written for parents to use with their children. And the Large Catechism was written for adults, including pastors, who were being "lazy bellies" just like everybody else. He left nothing to the imagination when he wrote in the introduction to that book what he thought needed to be done:

> Therefore, I appeal once more to all Christians, especially the pastors and preachers, that they not try to become doctors too soon and imagine that they know everything. . . . Let all Christians drill themselves in the catechism daily, and constantly put it into practice, guarding themselves with the greatest care and diligence against the poisonous infection of such security or arrogance. Let them constantly read and teach, learn and meditate and ponder. Let them never stop until they have proved by experience and are certain that they have taught the devil to death and have become more learned than God himself . . .[10]

---

[10] Martin Luther, *The Large Catechism, The Book of Concord: The Confessions of the Evangelical Lutheran Church*, eds. Robert Kolb and Timothy J. Wengert, (Minneapolis: Fortress Press, 2000), pp. 382-383.

Hmmm . . . I don't know how many of us will ever achieve being "more learned than God himself," but I wonder what it would be like if we really *expected* something to happen in our lives—and in our churches—because of the love and the welcome we have been given through Jesus. I wonder how many of us are really doing all the growing, all the learning, all the stretching we can.

In fact, now that you and Jesus have met, what in the world is holding you back?

Following Jesus into deeper water

Jesus was pretty clear, with the people he met, that life would be different as a result of their meeting. The man he met by the pool in Jerusalem had been sick for 38 years when Jesus showed up and healed him (John 5). Later, when Jesus found him in the temple, he told the man, "OK, now. Your life has been turned around. Now, go, and live your life like it matters. And try not to sin anymore."

Jesus loved people just as they were. But it was often, literally, within moments of that first meeting when he was inviting them to just drop everything and follow him. And, always, following Jesus led them into places they never dreamed of going before. That's how Peter found himself climbing out of a tiny fishing boat and out onto a stormy sea. Jesus said, "Come." And that was enough. The next thing he knew, Peter was searching for his balance on the waves and taking his first few shaky steps into adventure (Matthew 14).

Peter and his friends probably knew they were in for the ride of a lifetime the moment they met Jesus. They had been out fishing all night and hadn't caught a thing (Luke 5). That morning, Jesus borrowed one of their boats so that he could sit in it while he did a little teaching to the crowds on the beach. And, when he was done, he had a suggestion for them. "If you want to catch something worthwhile, guys," he said, "you have to go further out into deeper water." They looked at him like he was crazy. But they did it. And their nets weren't big enough for the catch they ended up hauling onto shore.

If we didn't know Jesus loved us so much, his call to follow him into deeper waters might sound more like a threat than an invitation. But we *do* know it. The truth is, Jesus couldn't possibly love us anymore than he does. If you're tempted to forget that, just look again at the cross. Remember that this is a God who always comes down. Remember that this is a God who gave everything there was to give so that we could live forever. We are saved through our *faith* in that God and not because of anything we have done to earn it. And this is what sets us free to follow wherever he leads.

The journey will look a little different for each of us, of course, depending on where your starting point is. For example, you might be a "wader" on this new adventure of faith. You're just sticking your toe in the water, curious as to what it would look like to take this journey but, if the truth be told, you are still a little unsure about what you think of this whole God thing. You've been to worship a few times or more. Maybe you've been to a church social event. You might even be a new church member. You're unsure about jumping in all the way. But, still, something seems to be happening to you. You think about God during the week. You feel like you want to give something back. You want to learn more.

It's weird, but sometimes you think you're even having fun.

Or maybe you're a "swimmer." You've made the plunge! You may not know all the fancy strokes, but you're learning. You are really trying to make the five faith practices—worshiping, learning, witnessing, serving, and sharing—part of your spiritual discipline. You *have* a spiritual discipline! There are some weeks you just can't wait to go to church. In fact, you are inviting all your friends. You're going to classes and trying to make prayer part of everyday life. You may be serving as a Kid's Klub leader or a worship leader. You may help out on a service project, building a home for the needy or working at the local food pantry. You see your volunteer work at the local school or as a Little League coach as a way of responding to the blessings God has given to you. It feels good to share your time with your church and you have even made a financial pledge. Your daily life is different because of what is happening in your spiritual life.

It is just possible, though, that you are a "deep sea diver." On the one hand, you can hardly believe this is happening. But on the other hand, you feel like THIS is what you were created for. Your faith is becoming more and more the center of your daily life . . . at work, at home, everywhere. You are trusting God with everything. You are working toward becoming a tither, giving away 10% or more of what you have every year to make a difference somewhere. You can't imagine starting the day without hearing God speak to you through your Bible reading. When God calls you to do something, no matter how scary, you pray for courage to say "yes."

And, just maybe, you are already a "lifeguard." You have the privilege—and the responsibility—of teaching others how to swim. You are a member of the preaching and teaching team, or the prayer team; you are serving on the church council or as a member of a church staff; you are part of the leadership at your church. You work hard to keep your skills up to par so that you can be there when someone needs your help. You know that the whole focus of our mission, as Christians, is all of those people who are "still ashore." *They* are the people we may not even have met yet. They are our neighbors. We know they have been watching us, and wondering what it would be like to get in the water. They probably believe in God, but they're not so sure that "religion" has much to offer. They are, most likely, a little afraid.

You know that we are not doing nearly enough to reach them. But that is our number one job.

None of us will move out into deeper waters because somebody yelled at us or threatened us or whacked us upside the head. But, knowing that we are unconditionally loved by a good and gracious God who always comes down to set us free—and who wades or swims or dives beside us—will give us the confidence and the courage to go places we would never otherwise dare to go. *Love* changes us. And I really do mean change.

Wrestling with the Word

1. The Bible is full of stories about people who encountered Jesus and were changed forever. Read Matthew 9:27-31. Who is it that meets Jesus is this story? What did Jesus do for them? And what was their response?
2. Maybe the all-time best story of how an encounter with Jesus changed somebody's life is the story of Paul. You have, perhaps, read it 100 times before. Read Acts 9:1-22. How is this an extreme example of the God who comes down in love?

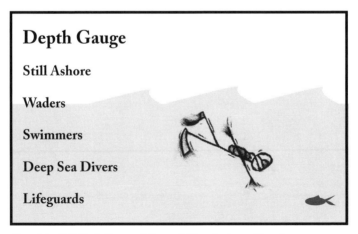

Depth Gauge

Still Ashore

Waders

Swimmers

Deep Sea Divers

Lifeguards

What was Paul called to do? Who do you think was more changed in this story, Paul or Ananias? Why? Have you ever had a "Damascus Road" experience? What was it like?

Thinking it through

1. Describe a time when you have been "whacked upside the head" by somebody carrying a Bible? How'd you feel? What happened?

2. Describe a time when you have seen somebody's life changed by an encounter with love—or a loving community? Maybe that person was you.

3. Where are you on the spiritual "depth gauge"? How are you doing at following Jesus into deeper waters? What is your church doing to help you—and others—go deeper? What waters would you like to explore?

4. How can you—and your church—make changes that will help you tell and live the message: God's love changes everything?

Talking it over

God of heaven and earth, you are truly the Lord of our lives. Your welcome has gladdened our hearts. Your love has changed us. Give us the courage to follow you, now, wherever you lead. Help us grow closer to you and clearer about what you are calling us to do . . . and to be. Make us more and more like you every day. In Jesus' name. Amen

6

Everybody Has
Something to Offer

To each is given the manifestation of the Spirit for the common good.

    Paul, to the gifted people of Corinth
       1 Corinthians 12:4-7

There is no other Word of God than that which is given all Christians to proclaim.

    Martin Luther, *Pagan Servitude of the Church*

Be responsible for your play on the field.

    Cal Ripkin Jr., *The Only Way I Know*, Viking Press, 1997

Many years ago I made an appointment to visit a new family who had been worshipping with us for a couple of weeks. It was my job, back then, to personally welcome each new family and spend some time trying to help them discern their gifts, so that they could go to work using those gifts to make a difference in the congregation. When the appointed time came, I arrived on schedule and walked up the steps to the front door. The door was slightly ajar, as though those inside were eagerly awaiting my visit. I could detect the warm smell of freshly baked cookies, no doubt also prepared with me in mind. There was a bustle of expectation within the house, I could sense, if not see. These guys had been waiting for me.

I rang the doorbell and set off a flurry of movement. Little bodies jumped up from where they had been trying quietly to play. Little feet came scurrying up and down the stairs to meet me. The oldest was five and his little sister was three. I imagined them tripping over one another to get to the door first. I smiled in anticipation of seeing their tiny faces peek out from inside the house. And then I heard a little voice ring out, "MOM, MOM!!! GOD AND JESUS ARE HERE!!!"

Being a pastor is the best job you could ever have. I don't know why more people don't want to do it. I talk to my own kids—and the kids in our church—every chance I get about becoming pastors some day. I hope every single one of our teenagers will consider going to a Lutheran college . . . and going on to seminary . . . to become pastors in this church. I love this job! But it is NOT the only one. And it is not the most important one. Not even close.

The renewal of our church hinges on a rediscovery of the important Lutheran idea that Everybody Has Something to Offer. The reformers called this principle "The Priesthood of All Believers." It is a concept we have *said* we believe in for 500 years. But I am not sure we have ever done a very good job of living it out. I know this may sound unkind but, frankly, I just don't see much evidence in our congregations that we really believe *everyone* is a minister. Instead, what I too often see are pastors who are overwhelmed and depressed because they have desperately been trying to "take care" of everyone . . . and people who are crabby or uninterested and bored because they don't feel like they have anything meaningful to do. I know this isn't the case everywhere. But, in a lot of our congregations, it is time for us to throw out our tired old images of "pastor" and "laity" to make way for something bold and fresh. It is time for each of us to hear God's call in a new way. And, make no mistake, God's call comes to us all.

The real heroes

I don't know how it got started, this idea that pastors are the only—or the most important—ministers in a church. But it is a pretty popular idea. Even a lot of pastors have it. In fact, I had a conversation with a pastor who had recently left her congregation to take an administrative position somewhere else in the church and, with tears in her eyes, she told me about how much she missed being the pastor of a congregation. "You know what I mean," she said. "I miss the way, when I used to walk into a room for a meeting or for worship or whatever, everyone would say, 'OK, we can get started now . . . the pastor's here.'"

Who started this?!? There is this crazy idea out there that somehow church "starts" when the pastor says so. Or that you can't *have* church if there's no pastor. If that were true, then all those churches out there who are "between" pastors or have a "part time" pastor or "share" a pastor or will never have a pastor . . . aren't real churches at all. And you and I both know that's not true. Where did this wacky idea come from?!? Well, I don't know. And I don't know why it continues to be this way in so many churches. But, I know one thing for sure; it is *not* in the Bible.

The REAL heroes in the biblical story are the ones whose names we don't even know. There is the little boy who shared his lunch and gave Jesus the bread and fish he needed to feed 5,000 people (John 6). There is the man nobody else would go near because they thought he was possessed by 1,000 demons. After Jesus healed him, he sent the guy out to spread the good news, and he went, becoming the first true evangelist (Mark 5). And then, of course, there is that woman who appeared at the end of Jesus' life and did something so insanely and extravagantly *loving* for him that tears filled his eyes. WHEREVER THE STORY ABOUT ME IS TOLD IN THE WHOLE WORLD, IT WILL BE TOLD IN HER HONOR, Jesus said (Matthew 26). And it is true: The real heroes in the Bible story are amazing, "regular" people who changed everything and turned the world upside down. They are the ones whose names we don't even know.

On the other hand, the disciples (you know, Peter and John and Andrew and all those guys with *names*) consistently got just as much *wrong* as they got right. And this continued even after Jesus put them in charge of things. Right up until the end they were arguing about whether or not Jesus came for *everybody*.

We know, of course, that he did. But it took them an awful long time, and a LOT of evidence, to see it, too (Acts 15). The point is that, right from the start, God has always called very ordinary people into ministry. And no *one* of them was more important than any other.

A pastor's job

There is nothing at all in the Bible that would support the idea that pastors are supposed to be the only ministers—or even the most important ones—in the church. In fact, Paul goes out of his way to help us imagine the church as a human body, where each single part is just as important as every other (1 Corinthians 12). That may be one reason our primary confessional document, as Lutherans, doesn't really even say much about those who are called to the office of pastor. This is Article V of the Augsburg Confession called *Concerning the Office of Preaching*:

> To obtain such faith God instituted the office of preaching, giving the gospel and the sacraments. Through these, as through means, he gives the Holy Spirit who produces faith, where and when he wills, in those who hear the gospel. It teaches that we have a gracious God, not through our merit but through Christ's merit, when we so believe. Condemned are the Anabaptists and others who teach that we obtain the Holy Spirit without the external word of the gospel through our own preparation, thoughts, and works.[11]

That's it. That's all it says about the office of pastor. And frankly, these words all by themselves are not a whole lot of help as we're trying to sort out exactly what a pastor is supposed to do or what it means to be in ministry as the church enters the 21st century. But I don't think the reformers were trying to do that. The main thing Article V is concerned about is the God who always comes down. The reformers weren't really trying to paint a picture of what a pastor is supposed to look like. It was only the message of grace through faith that mattered. And Article V asks our pastors to help us never forget it.

The only other thing the Augsburg Confession wants to make clear is that pastors are not in a "state of perfection." All it would take is one peek inside of *my* house, any day of the week, to convince you of that. Just ask my kids. In fact, those 16th-century reformers were wise enough to say that when there is a perception that pastors or other religious "professionals" are different or somehow special, it gets in the way of everybody else's spiritual life.[12]

The reformers wanted everyone to know that pastors aren't perfect. And they didn't spend a lot of time fussing about what exactly a pastor's job is. But that does not mean they didn't think pastors are important. In fact, I'd like to suggest the reformers thought a pastor's role in our churches goes way beyond the old formula of "preaching the Word and administering the

---

[11] *Augsburg Confession—German Text—Article V, Concerning the Office of Preaching, The Book of Concord: The Confessions of the Evangelical Lutheran Church*, eds. Robert Kolb and Timothy J. Wengert (Fortress Press: Minneapolis, 2000), p. 40.

[12] *Augsburg Confession—German Text—Article XXVII, Concerning Monastic Vows, The Book of Concord: The Confessions of the Evangelical Lutheran Church*, eds. Robert Kolb and Timothy J. Wengert (Fortress Press: Minneapolis, 2000), p. 88.

sacraments." This phrase has been used so often it's hard to even know what it means, anymore. And I *rarely* hear it used to get at the full meaning the reformers had in mind. I'm pretty sure they were imagining something way beyond "just" preaching and presiding at communion. All we have to do is look at the lives of those Reformation leaders, many of whom were pastors, to know this is true. Remember that they regularly *risked* their lives, challenging both religious and secular authorities, leading their congregations into new directions, stopping at nothing to get the Word out to all those who had not heard it. In their day, making sure everyone got the gospel message about grace through faith was dangerous business. And this was a pastor's job.

The Bible offers another model for what a pastor's job should look like in a couple of little verses tucked away in Ephesians, chapter 4. Actually, the original Greek word used here is "shepherd." But most translators at work today have chosen to use the word pastor. And it is the *only* place in most translations where the word pastor appears at all, in either testament. So, we have to assume that what *this* passage says about pastors is important. Here it is:

> The gifts he gave were that some would be apostles, some prophets, some evangelists, some pastors and teachers, to equip the saints for the work of ministry, for building up the body of Christ, until all of us come to the unity of the faith and of the knowledge of the Son of God, to maturity, to the measure of the full stature of Christ.
>
> ⬧ Ephesians 4:11-13

The author of this passage seems to be making a statement about everyone who is called by God's people to a particular office—to leadership—in their midst. These people, including pastors, are called to these jobs for a single reason: To equip the people of God for ministry.

Our pastors have theological training and expertise that can help us think together about who we are and what God is calling us to be. They have made a promise to make it their life's work, no matter how risky or dangerous it is, to make sure we never forget that the God we know in Jesus is a God who always comes down. We ask them to lead us, courageously and creatively, in seeing what God sees and doing what God calls us to do. We need them to be people of vision and determination, faithfulness, and deep prayer. We need them to be willing to lead us on wild adventures into a new day, seeking God's heart and loving the people of God's world and trusting in God's promises. We need our pastors today more than ever. But they are not the only people God calls into ministry. And they are not the most important ones.

I don't know exactly when it happened that, as a pastor, I started thinking I was the biggest fish in the pond. And I don't know, either, when it happened that, as a member of a congregation, I started thinking that I should get to put money in the offering plate and pay somebody else to do my job for me. Who started this? And, if we're all depressed, no wonder! The Bible makes it clear that ministry is not just the pastor's job; It is something *everyone* is supposed to be doing. Everybody has something to offer. And, frankly, Lutherans ought to know this better than anybody else.

The priesthood of all believers

This is our thing, right? The idea that we all belong to a "priesthood of all believers" is, as you may know, one of the greatest gifts Lutherans have given to the body of Christ. We teach, in other words, that through our baptism we are called into ministry . . . every single one of us. And reclaiming this concept is a critical key to the renewal of our churches today.

Martin Luther began exploring the concept of a priesthood of all believers as early as 1520, in a document called *The Pagan Servitude of the Church*: "Therefore every one who knows that he is a Christian should be fully assured that all of us alike are priests."[13] Luther said a lot of outrageous things in his time and this has to be on the Top 10 list. See if you can read through the formal, fancy, 16th-century language to hear how really revolutionary his thinking was 500 years ago:

> Here we take our stand: There is no other Word of God than that which is given all Christians to proclaim. There is no other baptism than the one which any Christian can bestow. There is no other remembrance of the Lord's Supper than that which any Christian can observe and which Christ has instituted. There is no other kind of sin than that which any Christian can bind or loose. There is no other sacrifice than of the body of every Christian. No one but a Christian can pray. No one but a Christian may judge doctrine. These make the priestly and royal office. Let therefore the papists either prove other functions of the priesthood or let them resign their own. Shaving, anointing, putting on of vestments, and other rites arising out of human superstition do not convince us otherwise, even were they given by angels from heaven. Much less are we affected by the arguments of ancient use, the opinion of the majority, or of the authority which has been recognized. [14]

---

[13] Martin Luther, *Pagan Servitude of the Church* (more commonly called *The Babylonian Captivity*), *Martin Luther: Selections from His Writings*, ed.John Dillenberger (Garden City, N.Y.: Anchor Books, 1961), p. 349.

[14] Martin Luther, *Concerning the Ministry*, 1523, pp. 34-35.

If your jaw didn't hit the ground when you read those words, then you may want to go back and read them again. I think this is pretty radical stuff even for *today*. Every Christian proclaiming the Word, bestowing the sacraments, offering forgiveness and comfort and hope, praying and serving and giving themselves away in a sacrifice of love for others? Every Christian a *priest*? Especially when you remember that Luther was writing 500 years ago, in the context of the medieval Roman Catholic church, this was an earth-shaking and, some would say *dangerous*, notion. In a lot of places, even in our church, he would get in trouble for spreading these ideas around today!

Now you should know that, in addition to these wacky ideas about how ministry belongs to every Christian, those reformers did say a lot about making sure we do things in an "orderly" fashion. They weren't crazy about the idea of doing church in a careless or, worse yet, chaotic way. They wanted to be sure that *everything* we do communicates clearly the gospel message about a God who always comes down, and comes down to set us free.

But, friends, there is a really big difference between doing things in an orderly fashion . . . and having one person do everything. And, let's be honest, that's how it is in too many of our churches. As I travel around the country and ask people, "How many ministers do you have in your church?" The answer I get over and over again is, "One." And this has to stop.

We could do worse today, in our life together as the church, than to take a page from Neil Armstrong's personal diary. He was, you probably know, the first man on the moon. He could have cashed in big time, too. But you'll never find him on the talk show circuit or out stumping for his favorite politician or making cameo appearances in big-ticket space movies. In fact, the Smithsonian Institution had to beg him for an interview. He finally agreed to do it as long as *they* agreed not to film it.

He is notoriously camera shy. But, here's why: Armstrong doesn't want his own reputation to take away from the contributions of thousands of people who worked behind the scenes, for decades, to make his achievement possible. He says he knows that nothing that huge could ever have been the work of just one individual. It only happened because every single person who worked on the project, from those who dreamed it all up to those who welded the ship together, knew they had something important to offer.

As radical as . . . Martin Luther

This great Lutheran idea that every Christian belongs to a "priesthood of all believers" is critical to the health, vitality, and renewal of our churches. It is our safeguard against ever thinking that any *one* of us is the only one who matters. It is a challenge to create communities of faith where people are responsible for their own spiritual lives; and where we care for and pray with one another. It is an invitation to be God's people in the world, making a difference everywhere we go. We each have been given gifts to share. We each have been given a job to do. A *pastor's* job is to lead God's people into the freedom Christ died for . . . to spark our imaginations so that we might be able to get a glimpse of what God is up to in this world . . . to call us into the future God has in store for us . . . to challenge us to follow wherever the Spirit leads . . . and to equip us to do what God calls us to do. *A pastor's job, in a word, is to help us become who we are: members of a priesthood of all believers.* And our job, as the baptized people of God, is to get busy . . . at church, at home, at work, in the community, and wherever God sends us . . . being God's people and doing what God leads us to do.

This may be a hard idea for some of us to get too excited about. Some of us are used to being a part of a congregation where the pastor's job is, let's be honest, to take care of us.

We may resist what is essentially a challenge to step up to the plate and take responsibility for our own spiritual lives, our family's spiritual life, and our church's life. Forgive me if this sounds too harsh but many of us come to church like we go to a baseball game. We never actually play the game at home. We don't necessarily teach it to our children. But we expect all the players out on the field, come game day, to play their hearts out so that we are entertained. We cheer when they do well and we boo when they don't. And we *always* complain about how much they get paid. Getting used to the idea that ministry is something we are *all* supposed to be doing is going to be tough for some of us who aren't used to imagining ourselves as ministers.

> **"For you were called to freedom, brothers and sisters; only do not use your freedom as an opportunity for self-indulgence, but through love become slaves to one another."**
> —**Galatians 5:13**

But it is going to be just as hard for some of us who are pastors. Many pastors have a difficult time understanding that their job really is not to "do" ministry. Most of them like doing it. They like preaching and teaching and praying with people. They like visiting those in need and comforting those who are grieving and counseling those who are confused. They like writing newsletter articles and leading worship and showing up at every meeting to keep the work of the church moving along. Most pastors are even pretty good at some of those things. But as long as our pastors keep *doing* all the ministry, everyone else will think it is all the pastor's job. And, it's not. That is OUR job, together as God's people. The pastor's job is to encourage and equip US to do these things.

As new as . . . the book of Acts

Besides, if the pastor is the only person anybody ever sees lead worship or teach a confirmation class or preach a sermon or visit the sick, then it's going to seem pretty obvious that he or she is the only person who *can* do these things. And, even worse, if the pastor is the only person really doing ministry in *here*, in the church, then why would anybody who is not a pastor ever imagine they could do ministry out *there*, in the world?

In fact, what would it look like if we imagined the church as a *training ground* for God's people to practice doing ministry—every kind of ministry—so that they are prepared to do it in their homes, workplaces, neighborhoods, and wherever they are called to be about God's business? What would it look like if here, on this training ground, people—all of God's people!—were set free to learn how to teach and to preach, to pray and to lead, to encourage the sick and comfort the dying, to imagine new possibilities and take the initiative for making new things happen? What would it look like if our *lay leaders* saw themselves as coaches, teaching and encouraging and challenging people in our congregations to discover, develop, and use the gifts God has given to them for ministry? And, here's an idea: What would it look like if a pastor's job—a pastor's main job—was coaching the coaches?

This is a call to embrace in a radical new way what is, in fact, a ridiculously old concept. I wish I could show you exactly what this looks like by giving you a hundred examples of how the priesthood of all believers is being lived out in our congregations. But I can't.

Instead, I can show you how it looked in the early days, when each and every Christian was expected to take responsibility for life in the church and for the church's mission in the world:

Awe came upon everyone, because many wonders and signs were being done by the apostles. All who believed were together and had all things in common; they would sell their possessions and goods and distribute the proceeds to all, as any had need. Day by day, as they spent much time together in the temple, they broke bread at home and ate their food with glad and generous hearts, praising God and having the goodwill of all the people. And day by day the Lord added to their number those who were being saved.

⋘⋙   Acts 2:43-47

The renewal of our churches will not happen until we have a dramatically new understanding of the old truth that everybody has something to offer. This is going to take a courageous redefinition, in most of our congregations, of what it means to be a pastor. And it is going to take a rediscovery of what it really means to be the people of God. We will need our *lay leaders* to take the very first steps, deliberately and fearlessly, into this new way of being church together. And we will need our *pastors* to lead the way. It will be their job to help us see this new vision and know that it comes from God. They will have to help create the space where a new kind of ministry can emerge. And, as *God's people* through Jesus, it will be up to the rest of us to step into that new space, with confidence and certainty that this is what God intended all along.

Five strategic behaviors

This kind of dramatic and total transformation—*a sea change* —in the way we do ministry will not happen by chance. After all, we have said we believe in the priesthood of all believers for the past 500 years. Clearly, we need to take some strategic action together if we expect anything to really be different.

Five Strategic Behaviors

1. **Pray Always**
2. **Set People Free**
3. **Take Action**
4. **Expect Surprises**
5. **Be Hopeful**

And we need to be patiently prepared for it to take a long time. The fundamental question, though, is this: Are we serious about being a church where everyone has something to offer . . . or not? Courageous, prayerful, and deliberate action will be necessary in most of our congregations for anything to really change. We just may need to change the way we *organize* for ministry. We may need to dare to mess with our *structure*, so that it sets people free to do God's work rather than stifling every new idea (and new person) that comes along. If you're not sure about the structure you're working with, ask yourself this: What does it take for someone with a new idea to get permission to "go for it"? If you don't know . . . or if it takes you more than five seconds to answer the question . . . your structure is strangling the Spirit. But structure alone isn't the problem.

Even more important than how many standing committees a church has or how many people sit on the church council, are the behaviors that characterize the culture and climate of the faith community. A church that is determined to live out this fourth guiding principle, Everybody Has Something to Offer, will live together differently than a church that is determined to just do business as usual.

It might be helpful, as we think about the new day into which God is inviting us, to explore the way the church operated in the *early* days. The book in the Bible that tells us about that early church is called "The Acts of the Apostles." It begins with the disciples being given a vision of the good news about Jesus reaching the very ends of the earth (Acts 1:8). They didn't have any graphs, goals and objectives, data, or flow charts. I'm not even sure they had a map. But they did create the most successful movement in history: The Christian Church. How did they do it?

It seems to me that we can identify five strategic behaviors those early Christians exercised as they went about fulfilling the mission Jesus had given them. First of all, they prayed all the time (Acts 1:14). As God's people in this new day, let's agree not to do anything that is not steeped in *prayer*. If God isn't in it, it won't work, anyway.

Second, in the power of the Spirit, those early Christians took their freedom seriously. They knew Christ had set them free from any and every worldly authority (Acts 4:20-21). If we believe that everybody has something to offer, then we too will be committed to *setting people free* every chance we get. Got a good idea? Is it of God? In other words, does it spring up from the Five Guiding Principles? Then, go in peace and serve the Lord!

Third, those first Christians never hesitated to do what they thought God was calling them to do, no matter how scary or how hard. In fact, we should be able to expect people to *take action* out of their sense of call and their enthusiasm for the mission of God's church in the place where they serve. Nothing should be less appreciated than someone with a lot of good ideas . . . who never makes a move to actually make something happen.

Fourth, Jesus' first followers often got it wrong. They found themselves, again and again, faced with situations they hadn't expected and weren't quite sure how to handle (Acts 8:39-40). If, in our church, everyone has been set free and is actively making stuff happen, we know that we will experience occasional bouts of chaos, too. We will be *prepared to be surprised*. And, sometimes we're going to take a wrong turn. Sometimes, as we go, we will discover that God is calling us into an entirely different direction. Once in a while we will have a gigantic mess on our hands.

But, fifth, we will move forward, anyway, *full of hope*, knowing that all things will come together for good when we are putting our trust in God. Those early Christians knew: This is God's church. It was God's in the beginning. And God always finishes what God starts. We will need to trust that this is true (Acts 27:25).

Let the adventure begin

A renewed church, full of the Spirit and full of life, will be a church where everybody has something to offer. And *that* kind of church will be a messy place. In fact, we may be entering a time in our life together as church when we will have to live with profound uncertainty about all kinds of things. We may be wisest to just agree, up front, that this will be a time of great experimentation and innovation in our life together as church.

How *should* we organize ourselves, anyway? And what exactly *is* a pastor's job description? And what *does* it look like to create a community of people who care for and pray with one another, instead of being dependent on a pastor or other church professional to take care of them? And how *can* we develop a climate in our congregations where people really feel free to share the gifts God has given them? And why *can't* gifted lay leaders, properly coached and duly authorized by congregational leadership, share the Good News of a God who always comes down . . . even in word and sacrament?!? And what *will* motivate people to take responsibility for their own spiritual lives, constantly seeking out opportunities to learn and to grow?

Some of these questions are, admittedly, scary ones. They turn upside down every idea we have ever had about what it means to be the church together. But they are not new questions. They are at least 500 years old. Some of them are as old as the Bible itself. Will we have the courage, as God's people, to ask them? How committed are we to this bold Lutheran concept that we belong to a "priesthood of all believers"?

We ought to know, down in our Lutheran souls, that when any one of us walks into a room—at home or at work or at school—Jesus really *is* there. God is at work in every single one of us. Everybody has something to offer.

Wrestling with the Word

1. Read Jeremiah 1:4-10. This is the story of how God called the prophet, Jeremiah, into ministry. Notice how many excuses he makes for why he can't do this job! What does God say to him? What excuses have you been using? What do you think God would say to you?

2. Sometimes the things Jesus' followers did caused quite a disturbance. Read Acts 17:1-9. Notice what Jason is accused of in this passage. What did the people he was with do that created such a ruckus? Do you think it's OK for God's people to "turn things upside down" once in a while? Why or why not?

Thinking it through

1. So, how upset are you right now?!? Do you think we need to re-envision what it means to be a minister . . . a pastor . . . a member of the church . . . a follower of Jesus? Or do you think everything is just fine the way it is?

2. What ARE your gifts? Has anyone ever helped you figure that out? If not, ask yourself these questions. What do you LOVE to do? How do you like to spend your time? What do other people say you're good at? The answers to these questions may help you begin to figure out what God has gifted you to do.

3. When you think about the "chaos" that might occasionally be created in your church if people really are "set free" to do ministry, how does it make you feel? Does it make you excited? Or scared? Or a little of both?

4. Do you think the church will EVER be able to get past the idea that ministry is "the pastor's job?" What do you think would make it hard for us to do that? What do you think the benefits of really acting like "everybody has something to offer" would be?

Talking it over

Well, Lord, you continue to surprise and challenge us. We are so tempted to think we have it all figured out. And then you come along and show us that we don't. Help us dream new dreams and imagine new ways of being church together. Give us courage to go where we have not gone before. Give us eyes to see what you see in us. Fill us with energy and enthusiasm for the work which is set before us. Make us willing to follow you wherever you lead, in Jesus' name. Amen

7

The World Needs What We Have

Go therefore and make disciples of all nations . . .

⪼ The last instructions Jesus gave the eleven remaining disciples
    Matthew 28:19

. . . the world, the planet earth, is a criminal planet.
Scientists know that hunger can be eliminated on this
planet, while 50 million people—50 million—more than
the whole of Central America, die out of hunger or diseases
related to hunger each year. So I call this planet criminal,
and also asleep.

⪼ Jon Sobrino, El Savadoran Jesuit priest
    Remarks presented at events commemorating the 20th
    anniversary of martyrdom of four U.S. churchwomen

I will take the ring.

⪼ Frodo Baggins
    The Fellowship of the Ring, by J. R. R. Tolkien

Have you seen this bumper sticker? I saw it on the back of a
beat up old Volkswagen, but I do not think the driver was refer-
ring to the kind of car he was driving. "Where are we going," it
said, "and why am I in this handbasket?" It's hard not to feel that
way about things, sometimes.

I don't know how scientific it was, but I recently saw the
results of a survey somewhere showing that kids think two of the
most important people in the world are George W. Bush and
Osama bin Laden. Mom and Dad rounded out the top four.

God was number five. "My cat," the garbage man, Jerry Springer, and Britney Spears all made the list, too. Jesus was way down at number 24 What a crazy world we're living in.

Silence is not an option

Miss Barett was my second-grade teacher—and I loved her—but she seemed to be about 100 years old. And that is just way too old to be teaching 7- and 8-year-olds. She never lost her temper with us, never yelled, never sent anyone to the principal's office. But she very rarely had much control over the classroom. Two of the boys were the ringleaders. They'd talk out of turn and fall off their chairs and crack stupid jokes in the middle of class. Miss Barett would try to get our attention over the giggling, shuffling, whispering noise. "Remember, children," she'd say in a creaky voice as loud as she could muster—which was never loud enough—"silence is golden." I always felt so bad for her. And I really did wish everybody would just be quiet and pay attention and let the poor woman off the hook. But, as much as I loved Miss Barett, she was wrong: Silence is not always golden.

Take, for example, that first Palm Sunday. You can read about it in Luke, chapter 19. Jesus had spent three years traveling the countryside, healing and teaching and reaching people with the good news about a God who always comes down and inviting them to join up with him in a life of meaning and purpose. And he had finally arrived to the place he had been heading all along, the center of religious power, the main event: Jerusalem. He knew what he was going to find there. He knew that the religious leaders were about as mad at him as they could possibly be. He had taken on the establishment and challenged the status quo. He had been hanging around with ALL the wrong people . . . and saying that was what God *wanted* him to do. Jesus knew he was walking right into a hornet's nest, into the belly of the whale, into a firestorm. And so, as he approached the edge of town and saw the crowds waiting for him, *smiling* crowds filled with children waving palm branches and young women dancing and old men singing songs. It must have made his heart swell. When he got closer, he could hear them shouting, "Blessed are you who comes in the name of the Lord!" And his eyes must have filled with tears. It was like God himself picked these people up and placed them on that road to cheer him on and encourage him as he traveled toward what he knew would be his last, terrible days. When the Pharisees started complaining, Jesus must have looked at them like they were crazy. "What do you *mean* they should be silent?! How COULD they be?! *God* put these people here! If *they* weren't here shouting my name and cheering me on, God would make these ROCKS start singing. Guys," Jesus said, "this is a *God* thing. And silence is not an option."

Well, after all these years, silence *still* is not an option. Jesus said, "You shall be my witnesses. Your job is to tell people about me and to invite them to come and get to know my Father. Your job is to feed my sheep and care for those in need and heal the sick and share with everyone who will listen to you the joy that comes from following me. Your job is to be my hands and my feet, to be the salt that *changes* the way everything tastes, to be a light that shines in the darkness of this world." In other words, Jesus said, "As the Father has sent me, so I send you" (John 20:21). That is our job. And terrible things happen when we fail to do it.

The knock on the door came in the middle of the night. We all heard it, even me, and my bedroom was all the way in the back of our small "shotgun"-style house. We got to the door at about the same time—my mom, my younger brother, and me. My youngest brother was 2 years old and still sound asleep in his crib. I was 11.

My mom answered the door as we watched, and we saw two men standing on our front stoop. One of the men wore the uniform of a police officer. The other wore that of a pastor. My brother and I couldn't possibly have imagined the news that they were bringing, but I think my mom knew right away. The first thing the police officer did was to make sure he had the right house. He got my mom's name and then asked her if her husband's name was Carlos. She nodded her head. He and the young man in black beside him both stepped inside.

"There's been an accident," the police officer said.

He refused to tell us how bad of an accident it had been, which made us fear the worst. We were hysterical. The poor guy did all he could to keep his own emotions under control as he guided my mom through the steps of calling someone to come and stay with my brothers and me so that she could go to the hospital. We begged him for more information. We begged my mom to just let us go with her. We begged God to let my dad be OK. My mom did her best to pull herself together. The police officer did his best to offer some words of encouragement. He knew the real truth, of course, was that my dad had already died. And he was doing his best to help us get ready for it.

But that young man in black? Well, he never said a word. Not a single word. He just stood there, in my living room, while my whole world fell apart around me.

I know now, of course, because I've been through it myself, that this poor young pastor was probably scared half out of his mind. He had most likely never seen anything like this before. He was, no doubt, a seminarian pulling an all night shift at the hospital. He didn't have a clue. Having stood in his shoes since then, I feel sorry for the guy. I really do. He probably went home that night hating himself. I wouldn't be surprised if he cried himself to sleep.

But that night was the beginning of 10 years of hell in my life. And I just need to say this again: Silence is NOT an option. Just standing there and doing nothing, when the world around you is crying out for help, is NOT an option. It's just not.

The freedom we share

Besides all that, Martin Luther said once that when you have had an encounter with the God who comes down to set us free, you just can't help yourself. That's what Peter and John said, too, in those early days after they were sent out on their gargantuan world-shaping, planet-crossing, earth-shaking mission. When the Pharisees ordered them to stop telling people about the God they knew in Jesus, their answer was: We can't. "Whether it is right in God's sight to listen to you rather than to God, you must judge; for we cannot keep from speaking about what we have seen and heard" (Acts 4:19-20).

It's like some kind of switch gets flipped in your heart when you really dare to look into Jesus' eyes and see what he sees when he looks at you. His love sets you free. It *changes* you. And all of a sudden, you understand WHY you have been given the gifts you have. Those gifts you have are not for your own sake. They are not for you at all. All of a sudden, Luther says, your "faith [is] truly active through love [Galatians 5:6], that is, it finds expression in works of the freest service, cheerfully and lovingly done." You find yourself daring to do the impossible, risking everything for the sake of those in need, wanting more than anything to be a part of whatever God is doing in the world, courageously giving yourself away.

Luther wrote that phrase—faith active in love—and a lot of other really interesting stuff in a 40-page document called *Christian Liberty.* In fact, I think this little book may just be one of the most helpful and important things those 16th-century

Reformers gave us. Because, in this little book, we discover why we are here. We see the *point* of it all.

God came down here to set us free *from* all the garbage in life that makes us miserable: sin, death, and the devil, for short. But we haven't just been set free FROM; we have been set free FOR. The words are 500 years old—but if you listen carefully, you will still hear them singing off the page:

> I will therefore give myself as a Christ to my neighbor, just as Christ offered himself to me; I will do nothing in this life except what I see is necessary, profitable, and salutary to my neighbor, since through faith I have an abundance of all good things in Christ.

> Behold, from faith thus flow forth love and joy in the Lord, and from love a joyful, willing, and free mind that serves one's neighbor willingly . . .

Luther was describing what happens in the lives of Christians: Jesus meets us and, all of a sudden, it's not about US, anymore. It's all about what we can do to make a difference in our neighbors lives.

Do you think Luther was right? I think my Aunt Gen would have thought so. She left me, and each of her great nieces and nephews, a little money in her will. It was like $500, I think. I don't remember the amount. In fact, the greatest gift she gave me wasn't the money at all. It was the fact that, because I was in her will, I got to see who else she left money to. Now, my Aunt Gen was never very wealthy. Teachers in one-room school houses never were. But she remembered in her will all those places and all those people she had prayed for and supported over the years. Boys Town. A shelter for runaway teens in Chicago. Her church. There was a whole long list of places that my Aunt Gen impacted through her giving during her life and helped, even through her death. I never had any idea. But, I wasn't surprised. She knew Jesus.

This is what the Christian life is supposed to look like: We are set free for a life of worshiping, learning, witnessing, serving, and sharing. We are set free to make a difference in the world. And I would like to suggest that what Luther says here for each individual Christian is also true for all of us Christians together. What we have here is a blueprint for what we are supposed to be doing together *as a church*. This is our mission. You could say it in a million different ways. I'll say it like this: We have been set free to be in action in this world for the sake of others, just as Christ was for us.

The strangest idea of all

Maybe the very hardest thing for us Christians to get our heads around these days is the idea that our church does not exist to meet our needs. This is, admittedly, a strange idea. We pay the bills. We do the work. It is only expected that we would, on a really bad day, imagine that what happens at church should make *us* happy.

Recently I met a man who is a well-intentioned and long-time leader in his church. Every Sunday morning, on his way out of worship, he says to the pastor, "Why don't we ever sing any of the good hymns?" Finally, his pastor invited him to make a list of the hymns he really likes. It seemed easier, I guess, to plan on just including these *good* hymns than it was to imagine seeing the poor guy leave unhappy every single week. Well, it turns out, when he turned in his list, there were just six.

We are funny this way. We talk about "my" church, as though the church were really ours, instead of God's. But God never intended for it to be this way. The church doesn't exist to meet my needs. It never did. Never will.

In Acts, chapter 1, Jesus gives his followers some last-minute instructions: "You will be my witnesses," Jesus said, "starting here in Jerusalem. And then out into the surrounding countryside, into Judea and Samaria. And, friends, then it'll be your job to take this message to the ends of the earth. I'll be with you in Spirit," he said. "I'll be there every single step of the way. But, guys, it's up to you."

Jesus was looking at eleven raggedy men when he gave those final instructions. And, remember, there were only eleven. The twelfth had deserted them and betrayed Jesus; he was nowhere to be seen. Those who remained were probably still feeling a little shaky after everything that had gone on. Their sense of community had been broken. They probably weren't sure they could even trust one another. They probably weren't sure they could trust themselves. If ever they needed something to be just about them, it was then.

But then, suddenly, they watched while Jesus was lifted up out of their sight. It took a couple of angels to show up and tap them on the shoulder to bring them back to earth. "So, what are you waiting for?" the angels said. "Get to work."

Thankfully, that is exactly what those eleven raggedy disciples did. Before long, that group of eleven was a little more than 100 (Acts 1:15) and not long after that there were thousands (Acts 1:41) and now YOU are here. And so am I. God works miracles when those who have been set free by Jesus get caught up in what God is doing in the world and give themselves away.

The church may be the only organization on the planet that exists entirely for the sake of those people who don't belong to it yet. In fact, as soon as we forget this and start making it all about ourselves, we stop being the church.

I don't know anybody who knows this better than the extraordinary people of Good News Lutheran Church in Fargo, North Dakota. This little church had a decent run over the years. But lately things have not been so good. Attendance was way down. Membership had taken a nosedive. Money wasn't too much of a problem for one reason or another. But those folks knew there was more to church than that. They did their best to turn things around. They called a new pastor and the council tried out every creative strategy they could think of to bring their church back to life again. But, in the end, they voted to close their congregation. They gave away their building and every cent they had to help plant a new church for a whole new group of people. The people of Good News knew that their congregation didn't exist to meet *their own* needs. They had a job to do. They knew they were supposed to share the Good News with people beyond their walls. There is no other way to say it than this: They got caught up in what God is doing in the world and they gave themselves away. And *that* is the church.

This is the noise we make

In the December 2001 issue of *Fast Company*, Keith H. Hammonds wrote an article titled "Business Fights Back: Continental's Turnaround Pilot." The article described the work of Bonnie Reitz, the senior vice president for sales and distribution at Continental Airlines when the World Trade Towers were attacked. Bonnie had already been pretty well known and respected for helping turn that organization around after years of decline. In fact, in her seven years at Continental, she helped raise the number of business passengers from 32% to 48% of its total mix, driving up its profitability. They were expecting $100 million a year in profits during the next few years. Then, September 11 hit. The airline industry was one of the first to suffer devastating losses in the economic aftermath of that tragedy. But instead of throwing in the towel, Bonnie Reitz helped set the tone at Continental, trying to help people see not just a challenge to the company, but an OPPORTUNITY.

She was determined to help move her company forward and even ahead of its competitors in the effort to win back the confidence of American travelers. She was interviewed by one business magazine after another during those first months after the attack, and the quote that made the headlines was this: "This is our time to lead."

I like the noise Bonnie Reitz made. It was bold and imaginative and hopeful. And, even if her company tanks, she has already made a difference. This is what God's people have been set free to do. This is what OUR freedom is all about. We are free, in Christ, even to fail.

The Bible says we are the "body of Christ" (1 Corinthians 12). That's a helpful image. It helps us think very clearly about how we each have a place in this community we call the church. It reminds us that we each have something very important to offer. But I think it says more than that. If we are really the "body of Christ," that means we are the flesh and blood *thing* that Jesus is using to get stuff done. That's what bodies are for, right? We use our bodies to pick things up and move things from one place to another. We use our bodies to GO places and to SAY things. We use our bodies to hug those who are sad and poke those who are lazy and vigorously shake hands with those who have done a really good job. We use our bodies to ACT. Therefore, if we are, in fact, the BODY of Jesus on this earth, then we are the people through whom Jesus wants to be at work in this world.

And, friends, Jesus never did anything that was just for himself.

If our congregations are a mess, the very first question we have to ask ourselves is this: Who are we here for? If we are all about ourselves, then we are going to be in trouble every time. I can't be at the center of my own universe or my family will disintegrate. And *we* can't be at the center of our churches, or they will crumble. Show me a congregation that doesn't share, and I'll show you a congregation that is dying. Show me a place that is willing to give its space away—during prime time—so that a new ethnic ministry can take root and grow in their changing community, and I'll show you a place where Jesus is alive. Show me a place that is willing to dissolve its endowment fund and put that money to use in a world hunger relief effort, and I'll show you a place where Jesus is alive. Show me a place that risks opening up its doors in the afternoon with a program for latchkey kids and in the evening for use as a homeless shelter and on the weekends for a community coffee house, and I'll show you a place where Jesus is alive. Show me people who put the needs of others— especially the stranger, the poor, the outcast, the sick, and the sad—ahead of their own every single time, and I will show you what the church really looks like.

Jesus isn't going to love us anymore if we do these things. He couldn't possibly. It is through our faith in him that we are saved and set free, not the good stuff that we do. This amazing truth fills us up, as God's people, and propels us into action. With the help of God's Spirit, we answer God's call to give ourselves away for the sake of others because we can't help ourselves. But, beyond that, it just feels great to be used by God to do good work. Nothing feels better than that. Nothing.

George picked me up from the airport to take me to a conference I was attending. We had about an hour to get to know one another. And the very first thing he told me is that he is a retired Sunday school teacher. He especially loved teaching fifth-graders. They are smart enough to be interesting but not old enough to be smart alecks, he said. These days, though, George spends his days caring for his wife, a once beautiful woman who has been slowly deteriorating from the ravages of Huntington's disease. She was first diagnosed 15 years ago. For the first few years, she was able to perform her daily tasks more or less as usual. But today she is unable even to dress or feed herself. She needs help going to the bathroom.

This is not how George imagined spending his retirement. He worked hard to get himself an education, back in the days when that was a rarer thing. He got a good job, working for a federal agency. He helped raise three children. He encouraged his wife to finish her education and supported her as she made a career for herself, too. George and his wife liked each other. They always have. They enjoyed going to hear the symphony and loved taking long walks in the park. They planned to have fun together once the responsibilities of work and family had eased up a little.

For the past 15 years, George told me, his wife has been saying, "Thank you." Every time he fixed a meal or changed the sheets on the bed or helped her to a bath. Every single time, for every single act of kindness, George would hear those words. "Thank you." These days, George said, these are about the only words his wife speaks. But, even when she isn't able to say them, he said he sees it in her eyes.

"I am a different man," George told me. "A better, more patient man. More appreciative. More alive."

Jesus said, "If any want to become my followers, let them deny themselves and take up their cross daily and follow me. For those who want to save their life will lose it, and those who lose their life for my sake will save it" (Luke 9:23-24). In fact, I have heard or read those words about a million times, but I don't think I ever saw the raw truth of those words so clearly until I met George.

Most of us think that we will be happier if we keep everything we have all to ourselves. We are afraid of giving our stuff—or ourselves—away. We're wrong. We have been set free from every single thing that makes us miserable so that we can share that freedom with others. All around us people are hungry and thirsty for the God we know in Jesus, the God who always comes down. And nothing we ever do will make more sense or feel more right or give us more joy that sharing that God with them.

This is the noise we make. It is a joyful, generous, hopeful noise. And it is loud enough for our whole crazy world to hear.

Wrestling with the word

1. God came to Paul one night in a vision, as he was battered on every side by people who wanted his head, and told him, "Do not be afraid, but speak and do not be silent" (Acts 18:9). The whole book of Acts is filled with stories about the courageous things Jesus' followers did to share with the world the good news of a God who always comes down. Read the whole thing if you can. Or at least read Acts 5:17-29. Ask yourself, what do you think motivated these people? What gave them courage? What gave them hope? What gives you hope in this crazy world?

2. Jesus and Peter had a pretty serious reunion after the resurrection. Peter had denied Jesus; they all had, really. They felt terrible. Jesus forgave them, of course. But that wasn't the end of it. Read John 21:15-19. Here Peter learns what comes after you are embraced by the love and forgiveness of Jesus. What does Jesus say that Peter needs to do? What do you think this means for you—and for your church?

Thinking it through

1. Have you ever really needed to hear a good word from somebody, and they let you down? Have you ever let the opportunity to share good news with somebody else slip away from you?

2. Being set free to serve means that you have been set free FROM all the things that hold you back, and make you afraid or sad or angry. If you—and your church—are really going to be set free to be a church FOR others, what do you first need to be set free FROM?

3. Who are the "others" in your world, the ones Jesus wants to use you—and your church—to reach? If you're not sure, ask yourself this: Who are the "strangers" in your community? Who are the ones in need?
4. What dreams do you think God has for your church? Be sure you're thinking big enough.

Talking it over

Mighty God! We are your people. Give us a new vision for our lives and for our church. Fill us with creativity and courage. Set us free from everything that holds us back so that we can really BE your body in this world. Put us to work, Lord God! Use us to make a difference. In Jesus' name. Amen

Afterword

Pretty gutsy, huh?!? There are approximately 5.1 million members of the Evangelical Lutheran Church in America. And every single one of us is in a unique situation. We live in different parts of the country and speak different languages and deal with different realities every day. And, here I am saying, "I think this is what it means to be a Lutheran."

What if I'm wrong?

Well, if it will help move the conversation along a little, I'm willing to take that chance. My life has been changed by the God I met in this church. And, yes, I think it made a difference that this church was LUTHERAN.

There was a time, about half way through our "redevelopment" at Cross of Glory, when we took the word Lutheran off all of our signs and brochures. It disappeared from our name. Now, I know a lot of churches are doing that these days. And there are good arguments for doing it. We figured people wouldn't know what a Lutheran was, anyway, and it might just scare them off. Besides, all the really big churches around seemed to be doing the same thing. We did it for the sake of mission. But that is exactly why we finally decided to put the word back in.

I *want* people to know what a Lutheran is! Because I believe we have something important here, something that will make a difference. I believe that what we have to offer to the world, as Lutherans, is special. Each separate part of what it means to be a Lutheran isn't exactly unique. But the way we put it all together, I think, is. We confess our faith in a God who is revealed to us in the face of the One on the cross, a God who comes down here to set us free. Jesus is Lord! And because Jesus is Lord, everyone is welcome. Really. We also know that this love which is poured out for us changes our lives. One of the things we discover is that we have been given gifts to use, for ministry, and that each and every one of us has something to offer. Finally, we know that these gifts are given to us for one reason and one reason only, so that we can give them away for the sake of a world that desperately needs what we have.

It is critical for us, as a church, to be thinking together about what it means for us to say that we are God's people through Jesus . . . who also happen to be Lutheran. I hope that you will spark a lively conversation in your church about this question. I hope you will wrestle with these five guiding principles and disagree with them and even debate them in good old Martin Luther fashion. I hope they will spur you on to try to define in your own place, in your own time, what it means to be a Lutheran. I hope they will help you answer the question, "Just exactly who are we, anyway? And what IS it that God wants to be doing in us and through us?" Nothing else that matters much will happen until we do this.

That much I am sure of.

Five Guiding Principles

1. **Jesus Is Lord**
2. **Everyone Is Welcome**
3. **Love Changes People**
4. **Everybody Has Something to Offer**
5. **The World Needs What We Have**

Copyright © Kelly A. Fryer and Cross of Glory Lutheran Church.

For Further Reading

Martin Luther and Lutheran Theology

Altaus, Paul. 1966. *The Theology of Martin Luther.* Robert C. Schultz, trans. Philadelphia: Fortress Press.

Dillenberger, John. 1961. *Martin Luther: Selections from His Writings— edited and with an introduction.* Garden City, N.Y.: Anchor Books.

Gritsch, Eric. 1970. "Introduction to Church and Ministry," *Luther's Works,* vol. 39. Philadelphia: Fortress Press.

Lohse, Bernhard. 1999. *Martin Luther's Theology: Its Historical and Systematic Development.* Roy A. Harrisville, trans. Minneapolis: Fortress Press.

Lull, Timothy. 1999. *My Conversations with Martin Luther.* Minneapolis: Augsburg Fortress.

Lull, Timothy, ed. 1989. *Martin Luther's Basic Theological Writings.* Minneapolis: Fortress Press.

Luther, Martin. 1989. "A Treatise on Christian Liberty," in *Martin Luther's Basic Theological Writings.* Minneapolis: Fortress Press.

_____. "The Babylonian Captivity of the Church, 1520," in *Luther's Works,* vol. 36. Philadelphia: Fortress Press.

_____. *The Book of Concord: The Confessions of the Evangelical Lutheran Church.* 2000. Robert Kolb and Timothy J. Wengert, eds. Minneapolis: Fortress Press.

_____. *Luther's Large Catechism.* Minneapolis. Augsburg Fortress.

_____. *The Small Catechism.* Minneapolis: Augsburg Fortress.

Oberman, Heiko. 1992. *Luther: Man Between God and the Devil.* New York: Image Books.

Mission of the Church

Bosch, David J. 1991. *Transforming Mission: Paradigm Shifts in Theology of Mission.* Maryknoll, N.Y.: Orbis Books.

Braaten, Carl. 1977. *The Flaming Center.* Philadelphia: Fortress Press.

_____. 1985. *The Apostolic Imperative: Nature and Aim of the Church's Mission and Ministry.* Minneapolis: Augsburg.

Guder, Darrell L. 2000. *The Continuing Conversion of the Church.* Grand
   Rapids: William B. Eerdmans.

Hefner, Philip. 1984. "The Church," *Christian Dogmatics.* Carl E. Braaten
   and Robert W. Jenson, eds. Philadelphia: Fortress Press.

Kirk, J. Andrew. 2000. *What Is Mission?: Theological Explorations.*
   Minneapolis: Fortress Press.

Nissen, Johannes. 1999. *New Testament and Mission: Historical and
   Hermeneutical Perspectives.* Frankfurt: Peter Lang.

Russell, Keith A. 1994. *In Search of the Church: New Testament Images for
   Tomorrow's Congregations.* New York: Alban Institute.

Scherer, James A. "Luther and Mission: A Rich but Untested Potential."
   Missio Apostolica: Journal of the Lutheran Society for Missiology 2 (May
   1994): 17-24. Reprinted in *Luther Digest: An Annual Abridgment of
   Luther Studies* (vol. 5, 1997): 62-68.

Van Engen, Charles Edward. 1991. *God's Missionary People: Rethinking the
   Purpose of the Local Church.* Grand Rapids: Baker Books.

Van Gelder, Craig. 2000. *The Essence of the Church: A Community Created
   by the Spirit.* Grand Rapids: Baker Books.

Congregational Renewal

Bandy, Thomas G. 1998. *Moving off the Map: A Field Guide to Changing
   the Congregation.* Nashville: Abingdon Press.

_____. 2000. *Coaching Change: Breaking Down Resistance, Building Up Hope.*
   Nashville: Abingdon Press.

Barna, George. 1993. *Turn-Around Churches.* Ventura, Calif.: Regal Books.

Bowen, John P. 2002. *Evangelism for "Normal" People.* Minneapolis:
   Augsburg Fortress.

Collins, James C., and Jerry I. Porras. 1997. *Built to Last: Successful Habits
   of Visionary Companies.* New York: HarperCollins.

Foss, Michael W. 2001. *A Servant's Manual: Christian Leadership for
   Tomorrow.* Minneapolis: Fortress Press.

Gibbs, Eddie. 2000. Church Next: *Quantum Changes in How We Do
   Ministry.* Downers Grove, Ill.: InterVasity Press.

Kallestad, Walter. 2001. *Turn Your Church Inside Out.* Minneapolis:
   Augsburg Fortress.

Kotter, John P. 1996. *Leading Change.* Boston: Harvard Business School Press.

Slaughter, Michael. 2001. *Unlearning Church: Just When You Thought You Had Leadership All Figured Out.* Loveland, Colo.: Group Publishing.

Strommen, Merton P. 1997. *The Innovative Church: Seven Steps to Positive Change in Your Congregation.* Minneapolis: Augsburg.

Sweet, Leonard. 1994. *Faithquakes.* Nashville: Abingdon Press.

———. 1999. *Aqua Church: Essential Leadership Arts for Piloting Your Church in Today's Fluid Culture.* Loveland, Colo.: Group Publishing.

Warren, Rick. 1995. *The Purpose-Driven Church: Growth without Compromising Your Message and Mission.* Grand Rapids: Zondervan.

OTHER LUTHERAN VOICES TITLES

Large-quantity purchases or custom editions of these books are available at a discount from the publisher. For more information, contact the sales department at Augsburg Fortress, Publishers, 1-800-328-4648, or write to: Sales Director, Augsburg Fortress, Publishers, P.O. Box 1209, Minneapolis, MN 55440-1209.

See www.lutheranvoices.com